Imaginative Prayer

Become immersed in the Scriptures of
the Sacraments

Carlie Anderson

Imaginative Prayer: Become immersed in the Scriptures of the Sacraments

Copyright © Carlie Anderson, 2024

First published 2024

Published by Carlie Anderson

Melbourne, Victoria

Email: imaginewithscripture@gmail.com

URL: http://www.imaginewithscripture.com

All rights reserved. Without limiting the rights under copyright reserved above, no part of this publication may be reproduced, stored in or introduced into a database and retrieval system or transmitted in any form or any means (electronic, mechanical, photocopying, recording or otherwise) without the prior written permission of the owner of copyright.

Cover design and map illustrations by Carlie Anderson

Imaginative Prayer: Become immersed in the Scriptures of the Sacraments

Anderson, Carlie

ISBN 978-0-6455542-2-9 Paperback

Acknowledgments

The following publications have assisted in providing the historical background knowledge of the imaginative prayer experiences.

Glavich, K., & Singer-Towns, B. (2017). *The Catholic Children's Bible*. Saint Mary's Press.

Hahn, S. (Ed.). (2009). *Catholic Bible Dictionary*. Doubleday.

Hahn, S. & Mitch, C. (2010). *Ignatius Catholic Study Bible*. Ignatius Press.

Catechism of the Catholic Church (2nd ed.). (1997).

https://www.scborromeo2.org/catechism-of-the-catholic-church.

Contents

What is a Sacrament? 2
Why the need for another sacramental resource? 4
Introduction to Imaginative Prayer 5
The Fundamental Principles of Imaginative Prayer 8
Introduction to the Gospel Writers 9

BAPTISM 11

Introduction to the Sacrament of Baptism 12
The Baptism of Jesus 14
Jesus Appears to His Disciples -On the Mountain Top 21
Paul in Ephesus 28

CONFIRMATION 35

Introduction to the Sacrament of Confirmation 36
Jesus Calls His First Disciples 38
Jesus Appears to His Disciples -In the Upper Room 46
The Coming of the Holy Spirit 54

EUCHARIST 61

Introduction to the Sacrament of Eucharist 62
The Lord's Supper The Institution of the Eucharist 64
Feeding of Five Thousand 71
Jesus the Bread of Life 79
The Walk to Emmaus 88

RECONCILIATION 96

Introduction to the Sacrament of Penance and Reconciliation 97
Jesus and Zacchaeus 100
Jesus at the home of Simon the Pharisee 107
The Lost Son Part 1-The Forgiving Father 117
The Lost Son Part 2-The Older Brother 124

What is a Sacrament?

The seven sacraments of the Catholic Church provide opportunities for individuals to directly encounter God at key moments of their lives. They remind us of God's involvement in our lives and, through the work of the Holy Spirit, the sacraments give us grace to help fortify and strengthen us on our faith journey.

According to the Catechism of the Catholic Church the sacraments "are efficacious signs of grace, instituted by Christ and entrusted to the Church, by which divine life is dispensed to us" (CCC, 1131).

A *sign* is something that can be perceived through our senses and which communicates to us a particular reality. Smoke, for example, is a perceivable *sign* that is universally understood to indicate fire. Sometimes, however, signs can indicate the existence of an invisible reality. For instance, a wedding band is a visible sign that communicates the invisible reality that a person is married.

In order to understand an *efficacious sign,* imagine the love shared between a parent and child. The *love* itself is invisible, yet through the senses, that love can be expressed and perceived–giving a hug, writing a letter, baking a birthday cake, or saying the words 'I love you'. These actions of love communicate and make visible the love that is shared between the parent and child. In addition, these actions have the power to reinforce, strengthen, and deepen the love that they express. Consequently, these actions, or signs of love, are considered *efficacious* as they make present in the lives of the receiver all that they signify.

The sacraments are *efficacious signs* because they bring about a change in the recipient. Take, for example, the Sacrament of Baptism which uses water as a sign of washing and cleansing. Through the grace received in the sacrament, the recipient is cleansed by the washing away of all sin. Within the Sacrament of Reconciliation, God's mercy and forgiveness is conveyed through the sign of the priest's outstretched hands over the penitent. The grace received through this sacrament also brings about the forgiveness of the penitent's individual sins.

Each of the seven sacraments were instituted by Christ and entrusted to the disciples, who established the Church. The sacraments provide an opportunity to strengthen and encourage faith development through the different stages of life. ***Baptism***, ***Confirmation***, and ***Eucharist*** are known as the sacraments of Christian initiation, because in receiving them a person becomes fully initiated into the Catholic Church. The Sacrament of ***Penance and Reconciliation*** along with the ***Anointing of the Sick*** are the sacraments of healing, through which we can receive God's mercy and forgiveness. The sacraments of ***Matrimony*** and ***Holy Orders*** are known as sacraments of service. These sacraments require serious discernment to determine how one can best live out the baptismal vocation to serve God and the Church.

The focus of this book is on the four sacraments that are most commonly received by school aged children: **Baptism, Confirmation, Eucharist, and Reconciliation**. These sacraments form the structure of the book and each chapter will begin with a detailed introduction to the sacrament.

Why the need for another sacramental resource?

The imaginative prayer experiences in this book have been created to support catechists and religious educators in their challenging task of preparing children to receive the sacraments. Although the family is considered the primary educators of the faith, parents are increasingly relying upon the expertise and knowledge of catechists and religious educators to provide faith formation for their children. Preparing children to receive a sacrament provides a unique opportunity to not only engage the receiving child more deeply in the Catholic faith, but also to enlighten the whole family. This book is not intended to be a complete sacramental program, rather it is a series of learning experiences designed to equip educators with the historical knowledge and context of key scriptural passages, whilst also providing personal and meaningful experiences for children and families who are preparing to receive God's grace through the sacraments.

The biblical passages explored within these imaginative prayer experiences have been specifically selected for the way they *make visible* many of the signs present within the sacraments of Baptism, Confirmation, Eucharist, and Reconciliation. These experiences will encourage children to not only learn *about* the faith through the sacraments, but to truly *experience* Jesus and his teaching for themselves. It is this ability to truly encounter the Lord, through the practice of imaginative prayer, that encourages participants to develop and strengthen their relationship with Christ in a unique and personal way.

Introduction to Imaginative Prayer

Imaginative prayer is an approach to reading the scriptures made famous by St Ignatius of Loyola. The practice encourages students to explore biblical passages through the use of their imaginations. Imaginative prayer enables participants to fully immerse themselves into a scriptural passage, allowing the Holy Spirit to guide their imaginations and deepen their understanding of God's Word. This approach can easily be incorporated into any religious education curriculum, with the classroom teacher facilitating the learning experience. The four-part process encourages students to imagine themselves as either a character within the biblical text or as an onlooker to the events taking place. Within an imaginative prayer experience the religious educator's role is to move slowly, providing the space and opportunity for the Holy Spirit to work. Let's explore each of the four stages of the approach.

1. Encounter

The initial stage of the process involves first exploring the historical and literary context of the designated passage, followed by a meditative reading of the biblical text. Ideally the educator would lead the class by reading aloud from a hard copy of the Bible with students following along with their own physical Bibles. Although some schools may not have the resources to implement this, it is crucial that students have opportunities to manipulate and become familiar with a physical Bible, therefore it is highly recommended that students use an actual printed Bible when encountering the Word. The teacher must begin by reading the passage slowly, allowing students the time to truly encounter the Word for themselves. The teacher will then read through the passage a second time to ensure all students are familiar with the text. This time of familiarisation is crucial in order for students to fully surrender to the imagination experience that will follow.

2. Imagine

The second phase involves students imagining themselves within the passage and being led through a scriptural meditation by the teacher. All five senses are drawn upon through the scriptural meditation and students are often amazed by the intricate details which they can imagine within what had previously been an unfamiliar scene. Ideally students would be given the space to lie down and completely relax their bodies and minds. Students could remain seated on their chairs, although lying down often enables a deeper imaginative experience. In this stage teachers must ensure they progress slowly. It is amazing what conversations and profound religious encounters can take place within the quiet moments of the meditation. Feedback from students suggests that the more they practise this form of meditation, the deeper their imaginative experiences become.

3. Discuss

The third phase of the imaginative prayer experience is completed through a traditional circle time discussion. Students form a circle, into which the teacher becomes a participant. The teacher poses questions to the class and encourages discussion about the time of *imagine*. Each imaginative prayer experience contains suggested questions to support educators in facilitating this discussion. All participation during this phase is voluntary and no student should feel pressured to share. What occurs within the *imagine* stage can often be extremely personal and as such students can feel quite vulnerable when asked to retell part of their experience to others. This time spent in discussion is very important. Sharing one's experience and hearing the experiences of others can not only solidify the encounter for each individual, but also provide encouragement and challenge for those who may not have fully immersed themselves in the experience. This honest sharing amongst the group commonly builds trust and strengthens bonds between the participants.

4. Contemplate

The final phase in the process provides students with their own time of contemplation, allowing each participant the time and space to reflect upon the passage and their own personal encounter with the Lord. This time is dedicated to work, where students choose to respond in whichever way seems most appropriate to them in that moment. This is commonly achieved through drawing, praying, writing a recount of the events, or even writing a letter in response to what was seen and heard. We often think of contemplation as time spent in silence 'thinking' about something. Although this may be an effective practise for some people, for children and young people to engage in reflection they need to be actively working. Therefore this 'work time'—which ideally will be conducted along with some quiet, reflective music—provides students with the space to really consider God's unique message for them and how it applies to their lives today.

Imaginative prayer is a wonderful way of allowing students to enter into the Word of God, regardless of cultural or religious background. This approach does not impose any interpretation onto the biblical text, rather it allows the Spirit to guide each student to imagine the passage for themselves. Although each imaginative prayer experience can take a significant period of time, the method allows the students to delve deeper into the Word, deriving meaning for themselves, and enabling them to grow in their own relationship with the Lord.

The Fundamental Principles of Imaginative Prayer

The following principles have guided the writing of all imaginative prayer experiences:

- Passages are read in their entirety, even if only part of the passage is explored within the imagine phase.
- Only one biblical author's work is explored within an imaginative prayer experience (passages are not merged).
- No conversations or events are added to the biblical passage. Therefore, meditations are created by using words taken directly from the biblical passage along with a series of exploratory questions to engage the senses.
- The spoken words of characters in the biblical text are not paraphrased but given in their entirety.
- No interpretation of the text is presented. Children are informed of the historical context of the biblical passage and given time to explore the message for themselves.

All of the imaginative prayer experiences have been written using The Good News translation of the Bible due to its understandability for younger readers. Although any translation can be used to conduct an imaginative prayer experience it is recommended to use a Good News Catholic Bible to ensure consistency of translation between the stages of *encounter* (when they first read the scripture) and *imagine*.

Introduction to the Gospel Writers

When reading a biblical passage it is imperative that students first gain an understanding of the author, their intended audience, and the purpose for their writing. Therefore, every imaginative prayer experience begins with an analysis of the historical context which includes a brief introduction to the biblical author. Below is a more detailed introduction to the gospel writers–Matthew, Mark, Luke, and John.

- **Matthew's Gospel** was written in approximately 80AD. The author is commonly believed to have been the apostle Matthew (a man referred to as Levi in both Mark and Luke's Gospel's). Matthew was said to have been a tax collector before Jesus called him to be one of his followers. Matthew wrote for a Jewish audience and often makes reference to the Hebrew Scriptures, which are commonly referred to as the Old Testament or the First Testament. His purpose for writing was to prove to his Jewish audience that Jesus was the Messiah that they had been waiting for.

- **Mark's Gospel** was the first of all of the gospels to be written, around 65-70AD. According to Christian Tradition this Gospel is believed to have been written by a man named John Mark from Jerusalem. John Mark was a Jewish man, believed to have been a disciple (meaning follower) of the apostle Peter. As a disciple of Peter, Mark's Gospel is understood to be based upon the eye-witness accounts of Peter. Many of the stories in Mark's Gospel are also included in the gospels of Matthew and Luke. It is the shortest of the four gospels and is thought to have been written for those living in Rome who believed in the divinity of Jesus.

- **Luke's Gospel** is known as the gospel for the poor and outcast because it includes many stories of Jesus showing love to those who were excluded from Jewish society. Luke was unique among the gospel writers as he is thought to have been a Gentile, meaning he wasn't a Jew. Luke wrote a sequel book to his Gospel called *Acts of the Apostles* which is also found in the Bible. Luke was a friend and travelling companion of Paul, having accompanied Paul on several of his journeys preaching about the Good News. The Gospel of Luke is thought to have been written around 70-80AD.

- **John's Gospel** is very different from the other three gospels. While the other gospels are very action packed, John's Gospel is much more spiritual and includes a lot more religious teaching. There is some disagreement amongst biblical scholars and historians as to when John's gospel was written, however it was likely sometime between 90AD and 100AD. This Gospel is believed to have been written by Jesus' apostle John, the younger brother of the apostle James, for Jews and Jewish Christians (those Jews who believed that Jesus was the Son of God).

Baptism

Introduction to the Sacrament of Baptism

The Sacrament of Baptism is the first of the seven sacraments and the beginning of a person's initiation into the Church. Through the work of the Holy Spirit, the sacrament prepares and strengthens the baptised to share in the life and work of Jesus so that they may participate in the Church's mission. The Sacrament of Baptism, therefore, is required in order to receive any of the other sacraments.

Prior to the beginning of Jesus' earthly ministry many Jews sought a *baptism of repentance* from John the Baptist at the river Jordan (Luke 3:3). The gospels tell us of people travelling to see John in the wilderness, sharing with him their desire to turn away from a life of sin in order to better live a life of faith (Matthew 3; Luke 3). John would then baptise the penitents by plunging them into the waters of the Jordan as a sign of cleansing and renewal.

The Sacrament of Baptism was instituted when Jesus himself was baptised by John in the river Jordan and the Holy Spirit descended, coming to rest upon Jesus' head (see *Baptism of Jesus*, p.14).

The Sacrament of Baptism is conferred either by full immersion into water or by the pouring of the baptismal water. During this time the words "[Name], I baptise you in the name of the Father, and of the Son, and of the Holy Spirit" are spoken by the minister of the sacrament. The immersion of candidates into the baptismal waters by the minister symbolises their entrance into Jesus's death. As they rise from the water, they do so as new creatures reborn in Christ, united with him through his glorious resurrection from the tomb.

Baptism

The Baptism of Jesus (p. 14) is a perfect way to begin an exploration of the Sacrament of Baptism as expressed in scripture. The passage highlights the transformative power of the Holy Spirit. This imaginative prayer enables participants to reflect on the differences and similarities between the baptism of Jesus and what is commonly experienced within the Catholic Church today.

In *Jesus Appears to His Disciples-On the Mountain Top* (p.21) participants get to experience, alongside the disciples, a post-resurrection appearance of Jesus. In this account Jesus authorises the apostles to go out, baptising in his name in order to make disciples of all nations. This passage highlights the importance of baptism both in the formation of the early Church and the continued spread of Christ's message.

Within the passage *Paul in Ephesus* (p. 28), Paul converses with two believers about the differences between baptisms of repentance and a baptism invoking the Holy Spirit. In addition to emphasising the differences between these two types of baptism, this passage somewhat introduces the Sacrament of Confirmation, for Paul is quite literally *confirming* the earlier baptism of the believers. As such this passage could be an ideal starting point for educators and catechists who are preparing confirmation candidates, as it shows the integral link between the sacraments of Baptism and Confirmation, which were, until the early Middle Ages, celebrated within the same rite.

The Baptism of Jesus

Matthew 3: 13-17 GNT Catholic Edition

In today's imaginative prayer we will be experiencing the story of Jesus' Baptism. We will begin by reading the passage together from the Bible before imagining the scene for ourselves through a guided meditation.

Historical Context

Today's reading comes from the Gospel of Matthew and takes place along the river Jordan. The Jordan river runs almost the entire length of Israel, beginning in the north, flowing southward into the sea of Galilee and continuing right through to the Dead Sea (see Figure 1 - Jordan River). In this story Jesus comes to meet his relative John at the Jordan river. The Bible tells us that John lived in the wilderness, that his clothes were made from camel's hair, and that his food consisted of locusts and honey (Matthew 3:4). John had become known to many throughout Jerusalem and the greater region of Judea as 'John the Baptist'. Many people travelled out to see John wanting to make a change, determined to turn away from their sinful behaviour in order to be better followers of God. John would then speak with the people about repentance before "cleansing" them in the waters of the Jordan river. This ritual of baptism was seen as the beginning of a new life for the baptised. While John was baptising people with water, he would teach and prophesy about the one who would come after him, saying that when he comes, he would baptise not only with water but with fire and the Spirit (Matthew 3:11; Luke 3:16; John 1:27).

Baptism

Figure 1 - Jordan River

Let us begin this session with a prayer of petition.

In the name of the Father, the Son, and the Holy Spirit.

Holy Spirit we ask that you help guide our thoughts and our imaginations during this time of prayer, Amen.

Encounter

Use a Bible to read the passage aloud to the class. Where possible, always allow students to hold their own Bible and to read along with you.

Now sit comfortably with your Bibles open to the Gospel of Matthew within the New Testament and find the large number 3 which represents Chapter 3. Then find the small number 13 which is called the verse. I will be reading Matthew 3: 13-17 aloud and I ask that you silently read along with me.

Read Matthew 3: 13-17 through slowly, ensuring that students are reading along

The Baptism of Jesus

[13] At that time Jesus arrived from Galilee and came to John at the Jordan to be baptized by him. [14] But John tried to make him change his mind. "I ought to be baptized by you," John said, "and yet you have come to me!" [15] But Jesus answered him, "Let it be so for now. For in this way we shall do all that God requires." So John agreed. [16] As soon as Jesus was baptized, he came up out of the water. Then heaven was opened to him, and he saw the Spirit of God coming down like a dove and lighting on him. [17] Then a voice said from heaven, "This is my own dear Son, with whom I am pleased."

We are going to read it through one more time. This time as we read through, I want you to try and imagine the scene and what is happening in the story.

Read Matthew 3: 13-17 slowly to the class before guiding the students through the scene

Baptism

Thank you for reading along. Now that you are familiar with the story, I'd like you to close your Bibles and find a comfortable place to lay down on the floor. We're now going to begin the meditation part of our prayer, where we allow the Holy Spirit to guide our imaginations. I will help to lead you through the process, asking you what it is that you can see, hear, touch, smell and even taste. Try to remain relaxed. If you get distracted, don't worry, just try and remain quiet so you don't distract others. Then refocus back on your imagination and allow my voice to guide you. Don't worry about where your imagination takes you or whether it seems appropriate. The idea behind this form of prayer is that the Holy Spirit is leading your thoughts and guiding you through your imagination, so try to trust the Spirit and know there is no right or wrong way to do this.

Imagine

Let's begin by closing our eyes and taking in three slow deep breaths. Breathing in and out, in and out, in and out.

As you breathe in try and imagine yourself resting on the banks of the river Jordan. Look along the river to your right, as far as you can see. Notice what the weather is like today, is it sunny, cloudy, raining? What can you hear as you sit on the river bank? What sounds can you hear from nature? Look along the river to your left. Is there anyone around that you can see? Are there any smells that you notice? You turn back and see a man standing at the edge of the water not too far from you. Pay attention to what clothes he is wearing, and what he has on his feet. Look at his face and hair. Who do you think he is? Whilst you watch this man you notice another man coming up to join him by the water. You recognise him immediately as Jesus. What does he look like? Can he see you clearly? What is he doing?

You watch as Jesus goes up to speak to the other man. You hear him call the man John. What is he saying to John? You watch John's body language as he says to Jesus "I ought to be baptized by you and yet you have come to me!" Does John seem happy, confused or upset? Jesus says something in return. Can you hear his words? How do you think Jesus is feeling right now?

The two men begin to walk into the water. Is there anyone else around that you can see? What can you hear right now?

Watch closely as Jesus' body and head are plunged down into the water. How do you feel as you watch this? As he comes up out of the water you look up. The heavens are opening. What can you see? What do you hear? How do you feel?

Look back at Jesus and John, how are they reacting to this? Are they shocked, scared, or joyful? Or maybe they seem unsurprised by what is happening, as if they knew this was going to happen all along?

You watch as the Spirit of God descends from heaven to rest above Jesus. What can you see? Could you describe the Spirit? What are Jesus and John doing? How are they reacting? Notice how you yourself are feeling? As you watch the men you hear a voice. Where is the voice coming from? Is it loud or soft? Can Jesus and John hear it too? Pay attention to what the voice is saying? I'll give you some time now to really take in this moment.

You might like to respond to the voice, or to go up and speak with Jesus and John. Just relax and allow the Holy Spirit to guide you.

Allow time for the children to respond

It is now time to leave the banks of the Jordan river and to say goodbye to Jesus and John. As you begin to walk away from the river, think about what God may have wanted you to understand about Jesus' baptism. Turn back around and give a final wave goodbye.

The time has come now to return to this room, so when you feel you are ready, begin by gently squeezing your hands, wriggling your toes, and then slowly start to open your eyes.

As you sit your bodies back up, we will say a short prayer of thanksgiving.

We thank you Holy Spirit for guiding our imaginations today and allowing us to experience God's word in this way.

I invite you now to speak aloud any prayers that you may like to share with the group.

Baptism

Allow a moment for spontaneous prayer

Now that we have finished the meditation, I ask you to please move yourselves into a circle so that we can have a discussion about what you have just experienced in your imagination.

Discuss

1- What did you notice whilst resting on the banks of the Jordan? What did you see, feel, smell and hear?

2- How did Jesus and John interact? How do you think John was feeling about Jesus coming and requesting to be baptized by him?

3- Can you describe what it was like when the heavens opened up? Try and include all of your senses.

4- What was the voice like that you heard and how did Jesus and John react?

5- How does your experience of Jesus' baptism compare with modern day baptisms that you might have experienced in Church?

Contemplate

Now to finish off we're going to take 10-15 minutes for contemplation, to really reflect upon the story of Jesus' Baptism. During this time you can respond to your imaginative prayer experience in a variety of different ways.

One response could be to write a recount or a snapshot describing in detail what you saw and felt during the imaginative prayer. A different written response might be to compose a prayer or write a letter to help you remember the experience at a later time. For those of you who would prefer to draw, focus your drawing on a specific moment within the imaginative prayer experience that stood out to you in a powerful or vivid way. As you reflect, in whatever way you would like, think about Jesus and John the Baptist. This event was recorded by three of the gospel writers. Why might it be important for us to understand what took place at Jesus' baptism? What can we learn from reflecting on this event?

*** Have some quiet reflective music playing in the background whilst children work***

Baptism

Jesus Appears to His Disciples

-On the Mountain Top

Matthew 28: 16-20 GNT Catholic Edition

In today's imaginative prayer we will be exploring a passage of scripture where Jesus appears to his disciples after he had risen from the dead. Jesus is no longer going to be with his disciples in quite the same way, and so he gives them a challenging task.

Historical Context

Today's scripture passage comes from the Gospel of Matthew. Matthew is believed to have been a Jewish man who wrote for a Jewish audience. The story we will read today is the very last account told in Matthew's Gospel. This event takes place *after* the resurrection of Jesus (his rising from the tomb) but *before* his ascension into heaven. In this short passage, Jesus appears to the disciples on a mountain in the region of Galilee where he had told them to meet him. This is a long way from where he had been buried just outside the city walls of Jerusalem (see Figure 2 - Jerusalem in the South and the region of Galilee in the North). Jesus tells the disciples that he has been granted all authority over heaven and earth. He shares his authority with the disciples and challenges them to go out, to baptise, and to "make disciples" of all nations. This challenge to spread the word of God and the life of Jesus through baptism has continued throughout the history of the Church, and continues today.

Figure 2 - Jerusalem in the South and the region of Galilee in the North

Baptism

Let us begin this session with a prayer of petition.

In the name of the Father, the Son, and the Holy Spirit.

Holy Spirit we ask that you help guide our thoughts and our imaginations during this time of prayer, Amen.

Encounter

Use a Bible to read the passage aloud to the class. Where possible, always allow students to hold their own Bible and to read along with you.

Now sit comfortably with your Bibles open to the Gospel of Matthew within the New Testament and find the large number 28 which represents Chapter 28. Then find the small number 16 which is called the verse. I will be reading Matthew 28: 16-20 aloud and I ask that you silently read along with me.

Read Matthew 28: 16-20 through slowly, ensuring that students are reading along

Jesus Appears to His Disciples

[16] The eleven disciples went to the hill in Galilee where Jesus had told them to go. [17] When they saw him, they worshiped him, even though some of them doubted. [18] Jesus drew near and said to them, "I have been given all authority in heaven and on earth. [19] Go, then, to all peoples everywhere and make them my disciples: baptise them in the name of the Father, the Son, and the Holy Spirit, [20] and teach them to obey everything I have commanded you. And I will be with you always, to the end of the age."

We are going to read it through one more time. This time as we read through, I want you to try and imagine the scene and what is happening in the story.

Read Matthew 28: 16-20 slowly to the class before guiding the students through the scene

Thank you for reading along. Now that you know the story I'd like you to place your Bibles down, find a comfortable place to lay, and close your eyes.

We're going to begin the meditation part of our prayer, where we allow the Holy Spirit to guide our imaginations. I will guide you through the process. Try to remain relaxed. If you get distracted, don't worry, just try and remain quiet and allow my voice to guide you back into your imagination.

Imagine

Let's begin by closing our eyes and taking in three slow deep breaths. Breathing in and out, in and out, in and out.

As you breathe in try and imagine yourself on a mountain top, looking out at the land surrounding you. What do you notice about the weather, the land, the view?

As you look around notice if you can hear any sounds. Perhaps you can hear the sounds of birds, or the wind, or even people talking in the distance.

Take in a deep breath and notice any smells in the air as you look out from the top of the mountain.

You have come to this mountain top with the disciples because Jesus had asked you to meet him here. How is it possible that you will see him again? Is it really true that he is resurrected?

As you think about these questions for yourself, look around for the other disciples. How do they seem right now? Do they look tired, worried, or at peace?

How are you feeling as you look out at the view, wondering whether Jesus will come to meet you as he had promised.

As you wander over towards the other disciples you suddenly realise that Jesus is there with you. *How* do you realise this? Is it a feeling inside of you? Can you see or hear him? How do you know it is him?

What is it like being near him again? Notice how you are feeling in this very moment.

You look around and notice the disciples beginning to worship Jesus. How are they doing this? Are they praying, singing, kneeling? What are they doing to show their love and admiration for Jesus?

Baptism

Are you also worshipping like the others? If so, what exactly are you doing?

Jesus begins to speak to you and the disciples. "I have been given all authority in heaven and on earth. Go, then, to all peoples everywhere and make them my disciples."

You stop and think about his words. What does he mean by *go everywhere*?
What about countries where there are no Jews? What about the towns ruled by the Romans? Surely he doesn't mean the places where people hate us? How are we meant to convince *them* to be his disciples?
As you ponder these questions you suddenly notice that Jesus is still speaking, "baptize them" he says, "in the name of the Father, the Son, and the Holy Spirit."
You continue to question yourself, wondering, how am I meant to baptize foreigners? Do I have the authority to baptize them in the name of the Father, the Son and the Holy Spirit?
When you look up you hear Jesus saying, "teach them to obey everything I have commanded you. And I will be with you always, to the end of the age."

Can you live up to this challenge?
How can you possibly teach the world everything that Jesus has taught you?
Jesus just said that he will be with you always, does that mean that he will continue to be with you like he is right now?
You look at the other disciples and see the expressions on their faces. How does everyone seem after Jesus' command? Do they look excited, scared, unsure?
Perhaps you have some questions that you want to ask Jesus, or maybe you want to share something with him.
Take this opportunity to go up to Jesus now and speak with him. I will give you some time together.

Allow students time to talk with Jesus

It is now time to say goodbye to Jesus and to set off on the challenge he has set for you. Take a final moment to say a proper goodbye to Jesus.

When you feel you are ready to return to the room, begin by gently squeezing your hands, wriggling your toes, and then slowly start to open your eyes.

As you sit your bodies back up, we will say a short prayer of thanksgiving.
We thank you Holy Spirit for guiding our imaginations today and allowing us to experience God's word in this way.
I invite you now to speak aloud any prayers that you may like to share with the group.

Allow a moment for spontaneous prayer

Now that we have finished the meditation, I ask you to please move yourselves into a circle so that we can have a discussion about what you have just experienced in your imagination.

Discuss

1- Describe what you could feel, hear, see, and smell at the top of the mountain.

2- How were you and the disciples feeling as you waited for Jesus? Did you think he would come?

3- What was it like seeing Jesus, and how did you know it was him?

4- How were you feeling after Jesus told you to go out, baptising and making disciples of all nations? How did the other disciples react?

5- Did you take the opportunity to speak with Jesus, and if so, what did you speak about?

6- Do you think Christians today are presented with the same challenge to go out and make disciples? Explain your thoughts.

Contemplate

Now to finish off we're going to take 10-15 minutes for contemplation, to really reflect upon the passage and the task that Jesus set for his disciples. During this time you can respond to your imaginative prayer experience in a variety of different ways.

One response could be to write a recount or a snapshot describing in detail what you saw and felt during the imaginative prayer. A different written response might be to compose a prayer or write a letter to help you remember the experience at a later time. For those of you who would prefer to draw, focus your drawing on a specific moment within the imaginative prayer experience that stood out to you in a powerful or vivid way. As you reflect, in whatever way you would like, think about how you might have felt being one of Jesus' closest disciples. Think about how he might be calling you to act in the world today.

** Have some quiet reflective music playing in the background whilst children work**

Paul in Ephesus

Acts 19: 1-7 GNT Catholic Edition

In today's imaginative prayer we will be exploring a time *after* Jesus had ascended into heaven. We will be reading about one of the many journeys that the apostle Paul made as he travelled around the world sharing the news of Jesus. In this story we will hear Paul talking to the people of Ephesus about different forms of baptism.

Historical Context

Today's scripture passage comes from the book called Acts of the Apostles, or simply the book of Acts. This book is the sequel to the Gospel of Luke, written by the same author, and it tells us what the disciples did after Jesus ascended into heaven. One thing we need to understand is that the word 'disciple' means *to follow*, whilst the word 'apostle' means *to be sent out*. Therefore, the disciples who were chosen by Jesus during his earthly life were given the challenge to become apostles and to *share* the news of Jesus with the world.

The apostle Paul, who was not one of the original twelve, was a friend and travelling companion of the gospel writer Luke.

Paul spent many, many years travelling across the world teaching and preaching about Jesus.

In today's passage we will hear that Paul goes to visit a Roman ruled city called Ephesus, while another friend of his, Apollos, was in a different town called Corinth (see Figure 3 - Ephesus and Corinth).

In this account the people of Ephesus, the Ephesians, talk with Paul about baptism and the Holy Spirit. The people tell Paul that they have never heard of the Holy Spirit and that their baptism was the baptism of John. The John they speak about is John the Baptist, who was a relative of Jesus and who prepared many people for the arrival of Jesus the Messiah. He was also the person who baptised Jesus in the river Jordan (refer to *'The Baptism of Jesus'* p. 14). John taught people to repent of their bad choices and turn away from their sinful ways, instead beginning a new life dedicated to God. The baptisms John performed were a cleansing of the old and a sign of a new life ahead. However, the baptism that we hear about in this passage, which is the baptism that Jesus proclaimed, is a baptism of the Holy Spirit. This was news for the people of Ephesus who had not heard of the Holy Spirit. This sacramental form of baptism is still received today by believers throughout the Christian world.

Figure 3 - Ephesus and Corinth

Let us begin this session with a prayer of petition.

In the name of the Father, the Son, and the Holy Spirit.

Holy Spirit we ask that you help guide our thoughts and our imaginations during this time of prayer, Amen.

Encounter

Use a Bible to read the passage aloud to the class. Where possible, always allow students to hold their own Bible and to read along with you.

Now sit comfortably with your Bibles open to the Book of Acts within the New Testament and find the large number 19 which represents Chapter 19. I will be reading Acts 19: 1-7 aloud and I ask that you silently read along with me.

Read Acts 19: 1-7 through slowly, ensuring that students are reading along

Paul in Ephesus

19 While Apollos was in Corinth, Paul travelled through the interior of the province and arrived in Ephesus. There he found some disciples ² and asked them, "Did you receive the Holy Spirit when you became believers?"

"We have not even heard that there is a Holy Spirit," they answered.

³ "Well, then, what kind of baptism did you receive?" Paul asked.

"The baptism of John," they answered.

⁴ Paul said, "The baptism of John was for those who turned from their sins; and he told the people of Israel to believe in the one who was coming after him—that is, in Jesus."

⁵ When they heard this, they were baptized in the name of the Lord Jesus. ⁶ Paul placed his hands on them, and the Holy Spirit came upon them; they spoke in strange tongues and also proclaimed God's message. ⁷ They were about twelve men in all.

We are going to read it through one more time. This time as we read through, I want you to try and imagine the scene and what might be happening in the story.

Read Acts 19: 1-7 slowly to the class before guiding the students through the scene

Thank you for reading along. Now that you know the story I'd like you to place your Bibles down, find a comfortable place to lay, and close your eyes. We're now going to begin the meditation part of our prayer, where we allow the Holy Spirit to guide our imaginations. I will guide you through the process. Try to remain relaxed. If you get distracted, don't worry, just try and remain quiet and allow my voice to guide you back into your imagination.

Imagine

Let's begin by closing our eyes and taking in three slow deep breaths. Breathing in and out, in and out, in and out.

As you breathe in try and imagine yourself walking around the Roman city of Ephesus. You and some of your friends have come together, having heard that the apostle Paul is on his way to visit the town. Look around you for a moment. Look at the buildings that surround you and the people. What do you see, what stands out to you?

Take a moment to notice if there are any sounds that you can hear.

Then, as you take in a deep breath, pay attention to what you can smell as you wander around the city.

As you look around you notice a man walking towards you and your friends. You immediately recognise him as Paul. What is it about him that stands out to you? What do you notice about his appearance? Are his clothes different from yours?

You watch as your friends greet him and begin talking with him and asking him questions.

While they are talking Paul turns to the group and asks "Did you receive the Holy Spirit when you became believers?"

You look at your friends, do they seem confused by the question?

Paul knows of your belief in Jesus, but what is the Holy Spirit that he is speaking about?

One of your friends answers Paul saying, "We have not even heard that there is a Holy Spirit."

Look at Paul's face, how does he react to this response? Is he surprised, confused, troubled?

Notice the tone in his voice as he replies saying, "Well, then, what kind of baptism did you receive?"

What does he mean? Are there different *kinds* of baptisms?

You look across at your friends, wondering if anyone will respond. One of the group speaks up saying, "the baptism of John."

You watch Paul again as he begins to explain to you the differences between John's baptism and that of the Holy Spirit. "The baptism of John," he says, "was for those who turned from their sins; and he told the people of Israel to believe in the one who was coming after him—that is, in Jesus."

You wonder what he really means by that. Does Jesus expect more of me than simply turning away from my old life and my old habits? Is there more that I can receive through the gift of the Holy Spirit?

As you continue to ask yourself questions, Paul offers to baptise you and your friends. How does he make the offer, is it through his words or simply a gesture that he makes? How do you and your friends react to his offer? Are you excited, nervous, or unsure about what is going to happen?

You see Paul raise his hands and place them down upon one of your friends. Watch your friend's face closely. What do you notice?

As Paul makes his way around the group, baptising them in the name of the Lord Jesus, you realise that you are next in line. Notice how you are feeling. Pay attention to your heart rate and any other sensations that you might have in your body.

Then, as Paul lifts his hands up to place upon you, take in a deep breath and feel the moment when the Holy Spirit is poured out upon you. Notice how you are feeling. Are there any changes either inside or outside of your body? Perhaps there are sounds that you can hear.

Try and really absorb the moment, allowing yourself to memorise this feeling. Paying attention to exactly what you are thinking and feeling in this moment.

It's not long when you begin to realise that your friends are not speaking in their usual way. Look over at your friends and try and listen to what they are saying, do you understand what they are speaking about? Take a deep breath and consider if you too are speaking in a strange way.

How are you feeling in this moment? Are you excited, terrified, confused?

As you look around you, focus your attention once again on Paul. What is he doing right now? Does he seem at all surprised by what is happening in front of him? How is he reacting to all that is taking place?

As you take one final look around the scene, you take in a deep breath.

The time has come to return to this room, so when you feel you are ready, begin by gently squeezing your hands, wriggling your toes, and then slowly start to open your eyes.

As you sit your bodies back up, we will say a short prayer of thanksgiving.

We thank you Holy Spirit for guiding our imaginations today and allowing us to experience God's word in this way.

I invite you now to speak aloud any prayers that you may like to share with the group.

Allow a moment for spontaneous prayer

Now that we have finished the meditation, I ask you to please move yourselves into a circle so that we can have a discussion about what you have just experienced in your imagination.

1- Describe the city of Ephesus? What could you see, feel, hear and smell?

2- What was it like meeting Paul? What was it about him that you recognised?

3- How did you and your friends feel when Paul started questioning you about your previous baptism by water? Did you understand what he meant about being baptised by the Holy Spirit?

4- Can you describe what it was like being baptised by Paul in the name of Lord Jesus? What was it like receiving the Holy Spirit?

5- How might this experience relate to the sacrament of baptism that take place in the Catholic Church today?

Contemplate

Now to finish off we're going to take 10-15 minutes for contemplation, to really reflect upon Paul's encounter with the Ephesians. During this time you can respond to your imaginative prayer experience in a variety of different ways.

One response could be to write a recount or a snapshot describing in detail what you saw and felt during the imaginative prayer. A different written response might be to compose a prayer or write a letter to help you remember the experience at a later time. For those of you who would prefer to draw, focus your drawing on a specific moment within the imaginative prayer experience that stood out to you in a powerful or vivid way. As you reflect, in whatever way you would like, think about what it must have been like to listen to Paul speak. Why do you think Luke decided to include this encounter in the book of Acts? How might this conversation still be relevant to us today?

** Have some quiet reflective music playing in the background whilst children work**

Confirmation

Introduction to the Sacrament of Confirmation

The Sacrament of Confirmation, along with Baptism and Eucharist, is necessary for a person's initiation into the Catholic Church. The gifts of the Holy Spirit, which are received through the Sacrament of Baptism, are *confirmed*, sealed, and stirred-up within the recipient through the Sacrament of Confirmation.

The Sacrament of Confirmation is commonly celebrated on or near the feast of Pentecost. The annual feast of Pentecost is a commemoration of the event when the Holy Spirit descended upon the apostles, sending them out to proclaim the Good News of Christ to all corners of the world. Similarly, recipients of the Sacrament of Confirmation are called to use the gifts granted by the Spirit to be faithful witnesses of Christ in the world.

The seven gifts of the Holy Spirit, confirmed and strengthened in Confirmation, are wisdom, understanding, counsel, fortitude, knowledge, piety, and fear of the Lord. These are gifts of grace supporting the recipient to be a true disciple of Christ, capable of speaking the truth and confronting the challenges of evil in the world today.

The imaginative prayer *Jesus Calls His First Disciples* (p.38) gives insight into what it was like for the earliest disciples to be personally invited to follow Jesus. Participants are encouraged to imagine the feelings and reactions of the disciples at the time, whilst also reflecting on what it means to be a follower of Christ in the world today.

Jesus Appears to His Disciples – In the Upper Room (p.46) is a passage many readers may be unfamiliar with. This imaginative prayer allows us to be present on the evening of Jesus' resurrection when he appears inside the upper room to his disciples who were

Confirmation

hiding in fear of the Jewish authorities. Jesus comes to bring them peace and breathes on the disciples, saying "receive the Holy Spirit".

As previously mentioned, the events of Pentecost correlate strongly with the Sacrament of Confirmation. *The Coming of the Holy Spirit* (p.54) is considered to be the birth of the Church. The events of the day inspired the disciples to go out and spread the Good News of Christ to the world. By entering the scene, participants can experience the events of Pentecost and reflect on the significance of the Holy Spirit within their own lives.

Jesus Calls His First Disciples

Luke 5: 1-11 GNT Catholic Edition

In today's imaginative prayer we will be immersing ourselves into the time when Jesus called his first disciples. We will first begin by reading the passage together from the Bible before imagining the scene for ourselves in a meditation.

Historical Context

Today's scripture passage comes from the Gospel of Luke. Luke was a friend and travel companion of St Paul the Apostle and was mentioned in some of the letters that Paul to different communities. Luke is the only gospel writer believed to have been a Gentile, which means he was not Jewish. We will read that this event took place on Lake Gennesaret which is the large fresh water lake located near Capernaum where a lot of Jesus' early ministry and teaching was done. The lake was most commonly called the 'Sea of Galilee' (see Figure 4 – Sea of Galilee). In this encounter Jesus will meet two brothers, named Simon and Andrew, who are fisherman. They also work alongside another family of fisherman–Zebedee and his two sons, James and John.

Confirmation

Figure 4 – Sea of Galilee, also known as Lake Gennesaret

Let us begin this session with a prayer of petition.

In the name of the Father, the Son, and the Holy Spirit.

Holy Spirit we ask that you help guide our thoughts and our imaginations during this time of prayer, Amen.

Encounter

Use a Bible to read the passage aloud to the class. Where possible, always allow students to hold their own Bible and to read along with you.

Now sit comfortably with your Bibles open to the Gospel of Luke within the New Testament and find the large number 5 which represents Chapter 5. I will be slowly reading Luke 5: 1-11 aloud to you and I ask that you silently read along with me.

Read Luke 5: 1-11 through slowly, ensuring that students are reading along

Jesus Calls His First Disciples

One day Jesus was standing on the shore of Lake Gennesaret while the people pushed their way up to him to listen to the word of God. ²He saw two boats pulled up on the beach; the fishermen had left them and were washing the nets. ³Jesus got into one of the boats—it belonged to Simon—and asked him to push off a little from the shore. Jesus sat in the boat and taught the crowd.

⁴When he finished speaking, he said to Simon, "Push the boat out further to the deep water, and you and your partners let down your nets for a catch." ⁵"Master," Simon answered, "we worked hard all night long and caught nothing. But if you say so, I will let down the nets." ⁶They let them down and caught such a large number of fish that the nets were about to break. ⁷So they motioned to their partners in the other boat to come and help them. They came and filled both boats so full of fish that the boats were about to sink. ⁸When Simon Peter saw what had happened, he fell on his knees before Jesus and said, "Go away from me, Lord! I am a sinful man!"

Confirmation

⁹He and the others with him were all amazed at the large number of fish they had caught.
¹⁰The same was true of Simon's partners, James and John, the sons of Zebedee. Jesus said to Simon, "Don't be afraid; from now on you will be catching people."
¹¹They pulled the boats up on the beach, left everything, and followed Jesus.

We are going to read it through one more time. This time as we read through, I want you to try and imagine the scene and what is happening in the story.

Read Luke 5: 1-11 slowly to the class before guiding the students through the scene

Thank you for reading along. Now that you are familiar with the story, I'd like you to close your Bibles and find a comfortable place to lay down on the floor. We're now going to begin the meditation part of our prayer, where we allow the Holy Spirit to guide our imaginations. I will help to lead you through the process, asking you what it is that you can see, hear, touch, smell and even taste. Try to remain relaxed. If you get distracted, don't worry, just try and remain quiet so you don't distract others. Then re-focus back on your imagination and allow my voice to guide you. Don't worry about where your imagination takes you or whether it seems appropriate. The idea behind this form of prayer is that the Holy Spirit is leading your thoughts and guiding you through your imagination, so try to trust the Spirit and know there is no right or wrong way to do this.

Imagine

Let's begin by closing our eyes and taking in three slow deep breaths. Breathing in and out, in and out, in and out.

As you breathe in try and imagine yourself on the rocky water's edge of Lake Gennesaret. You have come there, along with many others, to listen to a man named Jesus preach about the Word of God.

Take some time to feel the sensation of the rocky sand beneath your feet. Notice if the sun is shining or if the sky is cloudy, or raining. Pay attention to what else you can see. Can you see the other people who have been with you listening to Jesus?

Have a look along the shore, can you see any boats tied up? Perhaps you can see fishermen who are still out on the water, hoping for a last minute catch.

As you look around you, take in a slow deep breath. Notice what you can smell as well as what you can hear. Maybe you can hear waves lapping, birds singing, or even people talking.

This time as you look along the water's edge, find the boat where you can see two men washing their nets. What do you notice about them? What are they wearing? How old do you think they are? Do they seem happy, frustrated, or exhausted?

You watch as the preacher, Jesus, walks over to the two fishermen and begins to speak with them. You see Jesus as he climbs into the boat and they move the boat slightly further out into the water. Move yourself closer to them so that you can still hear what Jesus is saying. Take a brief moment to really listen to what Jesus is telling the crowd. Is he saying things that you understand?

Allow students time to listen to Jesus

When Jesus has finished speaking you watch him turn to one of the men on the boat and say "Push the boat out further to the deep water, and you and your partners let down your nets for a catch." Notice the fisherman's reaction. How does he seem?

You hear him respond by saying "Master, we worked hard all night long and caught nothing. But if you say so, I will let down the nets."

You wonder why Jesus would be telling them to go back out and fish at this time of day, yet you watch as the fishermen take the boat out further into the water. Although they are too far away for you to hear what they're saying, you continue to watch curiously as the nets are lowered back into the water. How do you think the fishermen are feeling? Do they seem hopeful of a catch, or unsure of why Jesus would have instructed them to lower their nets?

As you look out you notice the nets beginning to pull downward on the side of the boat. You wonder what could be causing the movement. Watch as the fisherman react, realising that the nets are indeed filling with fish. Suddenly the fisherman start calling for help from their partners in the other boat, gesturing with their arms that they need more help.

Confirmation

Can you see the others rushing to get to the boat in time? How is everyone reacting? Are they panicking, laughing, shouting?

In all of the commotion, notice how Jesus is responding? How do you think he is feeling?

In no time at all the fishermen have worked together and now both of the boats are full of fish. You notice that the boats are so full that you begin to wonder if they might sink.

As the fishermen and Jesus make their way back up onto the sand you think to yourself, where did all of those fish come from? How is it possible that so many could be caught?

When you look back around you, you notice that Jesus and one of the fishermen are now out of the boat and are standing quite near you on the sand.

Suddenly the fisherman falls to his knees before Jesus and says "Go away from me, Lord! I am a sinful man!" You notice the tone of his voice, does he seem upset, shocked, even sorry?

You see the other fishermen, a father and his two grown sons, walking towards Jesus on the shore, all of them looking amazed. Does Jesus look over at them?

Jesus then looks down and addresses the man kneeling before him, saying "Don't be afraid; from now on you will be catching people."

Notice how the fishermen respond. How do they each react to Jesus' words?

Does Jesus use words to ask them to follow him, or does he merely gesture his invitation?

Do the two sons turn to ask their father for permission to leave? Do they simply abandon their boats?

Do you notice any of the fishermen needing to take a moment to think about their decision or do they instantly respond to Jesus by following him?

Take a moment to think about how you feel right now? How exciting, yet terrifying, must it be to leave everything behind in order to follow Jesus?

The time has come to return to this room, so when you feel you are ready, begin by gently squeezing your hands, wriggling your toes, and then slowly start to open your eyes.

As you sit your bodies back up, we will say a short prayer of thanksgiving.
We thank you Holy Spirit for guiding our imaginations today and allowing us to experience God's word in this way.
I invite you now to speak aloud any prayers that you may like to share with the group.

Allow a moment for spontaneous prayer

Now that we have finished the meditation, I ask you to please move yourselves into a circle so that we can have a discussion about what it was like experiencing this story in your imaginations.

Discuss

1. Describe the scene by the lake. What could you see, feel, smell and hear?
2. What was it like listening to Jesus preach by the water? Were you able to hear what he was preaching about?
3. Describe what happened after Jesus asked the fishermen to drop their nets? How did everyone react to the nets filling with fish?
4. What did you notice about Simon the fisherman dropping to his knees before Jesus? Why do you think he did this and how did Jesus respond?
5. How might Jesus' call of his first disciples relate to the call he has for us in our lives today?

Contemplate

Now to finish off we're going to take 10-15 minutes for contemplation, to really reflect upon Jesus calling his first disciples. During this time you can respond to your imaginative prayer experience in a variety of different ways.

Confirmation

One response could be to write a recount or a snapshot describing in detail what you saw and felt during the imaginative prayer. A different written response might be to compose a prayer or write a letter to help you remember the experience at a later time. For those of you who would prefer to draw, focus your drawing on a specific moment within the imaginative prayer experience that stood out to you in a powerful or vivid way. As you reflect, in whatever way you would like, ponder why you think Simon, Andrew, James, and John all decided to leave their lives behind in order to follow Jesus. Ask yourself, is Jesus also calling you to be a disciple? What might discipleship look like for you today?

** Have some quiet reflective music playing in the background whilst children work**

Jesus Appears to His Disciples

-In the Upper Room

John 20:19-23 GNT Catholic Edition

In today's imaginative prayer we will be exploring a time after Jesus' resurrection when he appeared to his disciples. We will first begin by reading the passage together from the Bible before imagining the scene for ourselves in a meditation.

Historical Context

Today's scripture passage comes from the Gospel of John. Many believe that John was one of Jesus' closest disciples. He and his older brother James were part of the famous group of twelve apostles that were chosen by Jesus. The name 'apostle,' simply means 'one who is sent'. The Gospel of John is written in a different style that the other three Gospels and scholars agree that it would have been the last gospel to be written. In the passage we will read today, we will hear about a time when Jesus appeared to a group of his disciples in an upper room. It's important for us to understand where in the story of Jesus' life that this event takes place. After the crucifixion of Jesus, the disciples were fearful that they too may be arrested simply for being followers of Jesus, and so they were hiding out in a room within the city of Jerusalem (see Figure 5 - City of Jerusalem).

John tells us in his Gospel that Jesus appeared first to Mary Magdalene when she went to visit his tomb on the Sunday morning. Mary then went back to tell the other disciples and it was in that room, where they were hiding, that Jesus came and appeared to them. It is believed that this event took place in the evening of that same Easter Sunday.

You may have heard of a similar event which included a disciple by the name of Thomas, a man often referred to as 'doubting Thomas'. Thomas had not been in the room during the event which we will experience together today, and because of this he did not believe the other disciples when they told him that they had seen Jesus and that he was actually alive. It was due to this distrust and lack of belief that Thomas was given the name 'doubting Thomas'.

Figure 5 - City of Jerusalem

Let us begin this session with a prayer of petition.

In the name of the Father, the Son, and the Holy Spirit.

Holy Spirit we ask that you help guide our thoughts and our imaginations during this time of prayer, Amen.

Confirmation

Encounter

Use a Bible to read the passage aloud to the class. Where possible, always allow students to hold their own Bible and to read along with you.

Now sit comfortably with your Bibles open to the Gospel of John within the New Testament and find the large number 20 which represents Chapter 20. Then find the small number 19 which is called the verse. I will be slowly reading John 20: 19-23 aloud to you and I ask that you silently read along with me.

Read John 20: 19-23 through slowly, ensuring that students are reading along

Jesus Appears to His Disciples

[19] It was late that Sunday evening, and the disciples were gathered together behind locked doors, because they were afraid of the Jewish authorities. Then Jesus came and stood among them. "Peace be with you," he said. [20] After saying this, he showed them his hands and his side. The disciples were filled with joy at seeing the Lord. [21] Jesus said to them again, "Peace be with you. As the Father sent me, so I send you." [22] Then he breathed on them and said, "Receive the Holy Spirit. [23] If you forgive people's sins, they are forgiven; if you do not forgive them, they are not forgiven."

We are going to read it through one more time. This time as we read through, I want you to try and imagine the scene and what is happening in the story.

Read John 20: 19-23 slowly to the class before guiding the students through the scene

Thank you for reading along. Now that you are familiar with the story, I'd like you to close your Bibles and find a comfortable place to lay down on the floor. We're now going to begin the meditation part of our prayer, where we allow the Holy Spirit to guide our imaginations. I will help to lead you through the process, asking you what it is that you can see, hear, touch, smell and even taste. Try to remain relaxed. If you get distracted, don't worry, just try and remain quiet so you don't distract others. Then refocus back on your imagination and allow my voice to guide you. Don't worry about where your imagination takes you or whether it seems appropriate. The idea behind this form of prayer is that the Holy Spirit is leading your thoughts and guiding you through your imagination, so try to trust the Spirit and know there is no right or wrong way to do this.

Imagine

Let's begin by closing our eyes and taking in three slow deep breaths. Breathing in and out, in and out, in and out.

As you breathe in try and imagine the room where the disciples are gathered. It is late in the evening. Look around the room, what do you notice? Is it dark or are their candles or lanterns lighting the room?

As you look around the room you notice each of the disciples. Pay attention, are they sitting, standing, or perhaps even lying down?

Take some time now to walk towards one of the walls. When you get to the wall reach out your hand and touch it. How does it feel against your fingers?

Now take in a deep breath. As you do this, do you notice any distinct smells?

Pay attention also to what you can hear. Perhaps some of the disciples are talking. Or maybe you can hear people or animals walking by just outside of the room. Take a moment to really notice the sounds that you can hear.

When you're ready, look back toward the disciples, noticing how they are dressed. How might they be feeling in this moment?

They had stood by as Jesus, their rabbi/teacher, had been crucified and buried, yet earlier this very day Mary Magdalene had come and told them that Jesus had appeared to her outside of the tomb. She had proclaimed to them all that Jesus was no longer dead, that he had risen! How are the disciples responding as they wait here in the room?

As your eyes wander the room, you suddenly turn and see that Jesus is standing there among you. You look around wondering how he had come into the room when the door had been locked. Look closely at him, how do you know that it is Jesus? What is it about him that makes you so confident that it is really Jesus standing before you? You look around at the other disciples. How are they reacting to this incredible, unexplained appearance of Jesus?

How are you yourself feeling in this very moment? As you look into the eyes of Jesus, you hear him say "Peace be with you!" How do you respond? Can you speak? Do you embrace Jesus? What emotions are you feeling in this very moment?

As you try to understand what is going on, you begin to notice other disciples approaching Jesus. Do they seem confused, overwhelmed, excited?

You notice as Jesus begins to show them his hands and his side. You too walk closer to see for yourself. Can you see his bodily wounds? How does it feel to see Jesus with such injuries?

Jesus says again "Peace be with you". You watch as the disciples settle themselves to listen to Jesus. Do you sit down to listen? What is Jesus actually doing?

After a moment you hear Jesus begin to speak again. "As the Father sent me, so I send you". What must he mean by that?

Jesus has only just returned, and now he wants to send you away somewhere? Where will he send you? Why do you need to be sent?

As you ponder these questions you suddenly realise that Jesus is breathing upon you. His breath is shared with everyone in the room. What does it feel like to have Jesus breathe upon you? Why do you think he is doing that? Do you feel in any way different after receiving the breath?

You turn to look directly at Jesus, and as you do he begins to speak again to the group. "If you forgive people's sins, they are forgiven, if you do not forgive them, they are not forgiven."

So much is going through your head right now as you try to understand what is going on. You know that under Jewish law, only God can forgive a person's sin.

Is Jesus saying that his disciples now have the authority to forgive sins?

How is everyone in the room responding to this teaching? Is anyone asking questions? Does anyone look confused or excited?

You suddenly realise that this is your opportunity to speak with Jesus. You decide to move closer to be able to talk with him. Before you speak, take a deep breath in and allow your thoughts to be still. In amongst all that is happening, this is your chance to speak directly with Jesus. So breathe deeply and take this opportunity to have a conversation with Jesus now.

Allow students time to talk with Jesus

Unfortunately the time has come to say goodbye to Jesus. As you say your goodbyes, take another look around the room at what you notice. Take a final look at who is in the room with you, or perhaps notice any sounds that you can hear.

The time has come to return to this room, so when you feel you are ready, begin by gently squeezing your hands, wriggling your toes, and then slowly start to open your eyes.

As you sit your bodies back up, we will say a short prayer of thanksgiving.

We thank you Holy Spirit for guiding our imaginations today and allowing us to experience God's word in this way.

I invite you now to speak aloud any prayers that you may like to share with the group.

Allow a moment for spontaneous prayer

Now that we have finished the meditation, I ask you to please move yourselves into a circle so that we can have a discussion about what you have just experienced in your imagination.

Discuss

1. How would you describe the room where the disciples sat?

2. How were the disciples feeling before Jesus appeared?

3. How did Jesus enter the room? Did the mood in the room change after he arrived?

4. Describe the moment when Jesus breathed on the disciples. How did it make you feel?

5. Did you take the opportunity to speak to Jesus and if so what did you speak with him about?

Contemplate

Now to finish off we're going to take 10-15 minutes for contemplation, to really reflect upon this event. During this time you can respond to your imaginative prayer experience in a variety of different ways.

One response could be to write a recount or a snapshot describing in detail what you saw and felt during the imaginative prayer. A different written response might be to compose a prayer or write a letter to help you remember the experience at a later time. For those of you who would prefer to draw, focus your drawing on a specific moment within the imaginative prayer experience that stood out to you in a powerful or vivid way. As you reflect, in whatever way you would like, reflect on why you think John decided to include this particular story in his Gospel and why it has continued to be told for thousands of years.

** Have some quiet reflective music playing in the background whilst children work**

The Coming of the Holy Spirit

Acts 2: 1-21 GNT Catholic Edition

In today's imaginative prayer we will be going to Jerusalem for the Jewish festival of Pentecost to experience the coming of the Holy Spirit. We will begin by reading the passage together from the Bible before imagining the scene for ourselves through a guided meditation.

Historical Context

Today's scripture passage comes from the book of Acts which is the sequel book to Luke's Gospel, written by the same author. Luke was a Gentile (meaning non-Jew) and a friend of Paul. He wrote for a non-Jewish audience in order to demonstrate that Jesus came to save all of humanity, not just the Jews.

The book, Acts of the Apostles, tells of the actions of the apostles, meaning what they actually did, during the first few years after Jesus ascended into Heaven. This event is said to have taken place in or near the city of Jerusalem on the day of Pentecost. Pentecost is the English name for a Jewish celebration called Shavuot, or the feast of weeks, which is one of three special celebrations where the Jewish people would journey to the city of Jerusalem to worship God in the Temple. That is why people were there from different countries and regions throughout Europe and Asia (see Figure 6 - Visitors to Jerusalem at Pentecost). Shavuot is a celebration to commemorate the time when God gave the Ten Commandments to Moses at Mount Sinai.

Confirmation

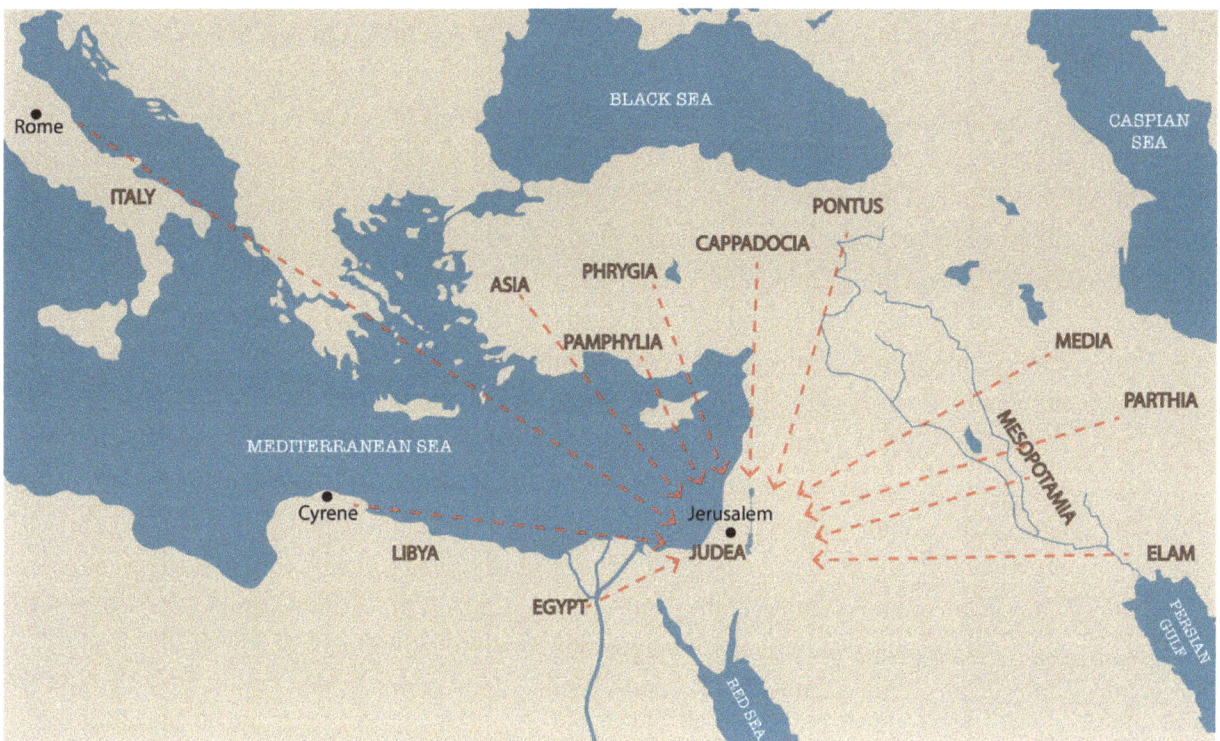

Figure 6 - Visitors to Jerusalem at Pentecost

Let us begin this session with a prayer of petition.

In the name of the Father, the Son, and the Holy Spirit.

Holy Spirit we ask that you help guide our thoughts and our imaginations during this time of prayer, Amen.

Use a Bible to read the passage aloud to the class. Where possible, always allow students to hold their own Bible and to read along with you

Now sit comfortably with your Bibles. The Acts of the Apostles can be found immediately after the four Gospels. Find the large number 2 which represents Chapter 2. I will begin by reading through a very long passage, Acts 2: 1-21 and ask that you silently read along with me. On the second reading we will focus our attention only on the first part of the passage, but it is very important to first get a fuller understanding of what took place.

Read Acts 2: 1-21 through slowly, ensuring that students are reading along

The Coming of the Holy Spirit

When the day of Pentecost came, all the believers were gathered together in one place. ² Suddenly there was a noise from the sky which sounded like a strong wind blowing, and it filled the whole house where they were sitting. ³ Then they saw what looked like tongues of fire which spread out and touched each person there. ⁴ They were all filled with the Holy Spirit and began to talk in other languages, as the Spirit enabled them to speak.⁵ There were Jews living in Jerusalem, religious people who had come from every country in the world. ⁶ When they heard this noise, a large crowd gathered. They were all excited, because all of them heard the believers talking in their own languages. ⁷ In amazement and wonder they exclaimed, "These people who are talking like this are Galileans! ⁸ How is it, then, that all of us hear them speaking in our own native languages? ⁹ We are from Parthia, Media, and Elam; from Mesopotamia, Judea, and Cappadocia; from Pontus and Asia, ¹⁰ from Phrygia and Pamphylia, from Egypt and the regions of Libya near Cyrene. Some of us are from Rome, ¹¹ both Jews and Gentiles converted to Judaism, and some of us are from Crete and Arabia—yet all of us hear them speaking in our own languages about the great things that God has done!" ¹² Amazed and confused, they kept asking each other, "What does this mean? ¹³ But others made fun of the believers, saying, "These people are drunk!"

Peter's Message

¹⁴ Then Peter stood up with the other eleven apostles and in a loud voice began to speak to the crowd: "Fellow Jews and all of you who live in Jerusalem, listen to me and let me tell you what this means. ¹⁵ These people are not drunk, as you suppose; it is only nine o'clock in the morning. ¹⁶ Instead, this is what the prophet Joel spoke about:

¹⁷ 'This is what I will do in the last days, God says:

I will pour out my Spirit on everyone.

Your sons and daughters will proclaim my message;

your young men will see visions,

and your old men will have dreams.

¹⁸ Yes, even on my servants, both men and women,

I will pour out my Spirit in those days,

and they will proclaim my message.
¹⁹ I will perform miracles in the sky above
and wonders on the earth below.
There will be blood, fire, and thick smoke;
²⁰the sun will be darkened,
and the moon will turn red as blood,
before the great and glorious Day of the Lord comes.
²¹ And then, whoever calls out to the Lord for help will be saved.'

We are going to read it through one more time. This time as we read through, I want you to try and imagine the scene and what is happening in the story

Read **Acts 2: 1-13** slowly to the class before guiding the students through the scene

Thank you for reading along. Now that you know the story I'd like you to place your Bibles down and find a comfortable place to lay down and close your eyes. We're now going to begin the meditation part of our prayer, where we allow the Holy Spirit to guide our imaginations. I will guide you through the process. Try to remain relaxed. If you get distracted, don't worry, just try and remain quiet and allow my voice to guide you back into your imagination.

Imagine

Let's begin by closing our eyes and taking in three slow deep breaths. Breathing in and out, in and out, in and out.

As you breathe in try and imagine the scene inside the house. It's the day of Shavuot in Jerusalem and the apostles have gathered together to commemorate the day. Can you see the apostles sitting down together? What are they doing? Are they talking, celebrating, reflecting? What character are you in the story? Are you one of the apostles, a visitor to Judea or a local watching on?

Now look around you, what can you see? Is the sun shining into the room or is it cold and dark? How many people can you see around you? Is anyone talking, if so what are they saying? Are you able to talk to anyone?

Pay attention to what else you can hear. Are there noises coming from outside? Are there people wandering the streets? What about your senses of taste, smell or touch, do you notice anything?

You suddenly hear a noise, like that of a strong wind blowing. It fills the room where the apostles are sitting. How do they react? Do they appear scared, worried or confused? Can you feel a wind blowing, or is it simply a sound you can hear? Look around you, what can you see?

Something that looks like flames of fire appear above those within the room, can you see this? What does it really look like to you? How are people reacting? How are you feeling? Are you terrified, excited, overwhelmed? Notice what you can hear, is there a commotion, is there stillness or are people going on with their day unaware of what's happening.

You notice that the apostles begin to speak in all different languages, are you speaking differently too?

Take your time to rest here in this moment, move around the scene, taking in all that you see, hear, touch and smell.

The noise draws a crowd from outside, what do you notice about those coming in. What are they wearing? What do they look like? Walk up to one of the visitors and stand near them, what expression do you notice on his/her face? Does the visitor seem excited, amazed, confused?

Continue to let your imagination wander the room. Is there anything that you can smell? Notice if there is anything that you can feel, such as what is under your feet? Can you talk to anyone?

You hear people ask "What is happening?", can you see the person who asked this? What do they look like? Do they seem concerned? You then turn to see a group of people laughing and claiming that the apostles are drunk.

Confirmation

Take a moment now and observe the apostles speaking in different languages. Do you understand what they are saying? What do you think they are talking about? Do they seem inspired, afraid, possessed? What do you think is happening? Do you agree that they are drunk? Why or why not? Think about your answer in light of what you see and feel in the room. Now take a moment to notice how *you* are feeling.

When you feel like you have finished within the scene, think about how the story might end. What happens to the apostles and all of those watching on? Think about how you might have felt if you were one of the apostles, or if you have been a visitor to Judea and had seen all of this take place. What can you learn from these characters that could help you in your own life? What insight into the scripture passage did your imaginative prayer provide?

The time has come to return to this room, so when you feel you are ready, begin by gently squeezing your hands, wriggling your toes, and then slowly start to open your eyes.

As you sit your bodies back up, we will say a short prayer of thanksgiving.
We thank you Holy Spirit for guiding our imaginations today and allowing us to experience God's word in this way.
I invite you now to speak aloud any prayers that you may like to share with the group.

Allow a moment for spontaneous prayer

Now that we have finished the meditation, I ask you to please move yourselves into a circle so that we can have a discussion about what you have just experienced in your imagination.

Discuss

1. Describe what it was like in the upper room, what could you hear, see, feel and smell?
2. What did the wind feel like and how did everyone react when it entered the room?
3. Scripture describes the appearance of something like tongues of fire? What did you see and experience in this moment and how did it make you feel?
4. What was it like for you when the apostles started talking in different languages? Could you understand what they were talking about?
5. What do you think happened to the apostles after the scene ended?

Contemplate

Now to finish off we're going to take 10-15 minutes for contemplation, to really reflect upon the story of Pentecost. During this time you can respond to your imaginative prayer experience in a variety of different ways.

One response could be to write a recount or a snapshot describing in detail what you saw and felt during the imaginative prayer. A different written response might be to compose a prayer or write a letter to help you remember the experience at a later time. For those of you who would prefer to draw, focus your drawing on a specific moment within the imaginative prayer experience that stood out to you in a powerful or vivid way. As you reflect, in whatever way you would like, think about the characters and events in this story and ask yourself, why did the author Luke think that the story of Pentecost should be known and understood? What might God be trying to tell you through this story?

** Have some quiet reflective music playing in the background whilst children work*

Eucharist

Introduction to the Sacrament of Eucharist

The Sacrament of the Eucharist is the source and summit of the Christian life. It is through receiving the Body, Blood, Soul and Divinity of Christ in the Eucharist that the faithful are fed and nourished to become more like Jesus.

The Sacrament of the Eucharist, along with the sacraments of Baptism and Confirmation, completes Christian initiation. Unlike Baptism and Confirmation, however, which can only be received once, the Sacrament of the Eucharist is offered at every celebration of the Mass providing ongoing spiritual nourishment and conversion of the faithful.

The gifts of bread and wine offered at Mass are consecrated by the priest using the words spoken by Jesus at the Last Supper. Then, through the power and work of the Holy Spirit, Jesus becomes truly present in the bread and wine which are now the Body and Blood of Jesus Christ. Although the physical form, appearance, and taste of the consecrated bread and wine may remain unchanged, it is the *substance* of the bread and wine that truly changes. This change that is enacted by the Holy Spirit is referred to as *transubstantiation*.

Understanding the events of *The Lord's Supper* (p. 64) is crucial to understanding the Sacrament of the Eucharist. In joining the Passover meal, where Jesus instituted the Eucharist, participants are able to gain an insight into the significance both historically and personally of Christ's invitation to eat of his Body and drink of his Blood.

Feeding the Five Thousand (p.71) is the only miracle, other than the resurrection of Jesus, which is recorded in all four Gospels. This event demonstrates Jesus' ability to feed and

Eucharist

sustain his followers through a multiplication of even the smallest of offerings. Participants are encouraged to reflect upon Jesus' actions in the passage and to consider how Jesus continues to sustain all the faithful of the Church through the Eucharist.

Jesus the Bread of Life (p.79) allows us to enter into a challenging, even confronting, passage where Jesus explains and clarifies his teaching on the Eucharist. This encounter will emphasise why the Catholic Church holds firm on its teaching of Jesus' true presence in the Eucharist.

The final passage exploring the Sacrament of the Eucharist is *The Walk to Emmaus* (p.88). Through this encounter with the risen Christ, we gain a unique insight into the structure of the Mass. It begins with the proclamation of the Word of God, followed by the breaking of the bread, and concludes with the sending out of the faithful to share the Good News of Christ with others.

The Lord's Supper

The Institution of the Eucharist

Mark 14: 22-26 GNT Catholic Edition

In today's imaginative prayer we will be imagining ourselves as guests at the Last Supper. We will be reading Mark's account, however other accounts can be found in Matthew 26: 26-29 and Luke 22: 14-23. We will begin by reading the passage together from the Bible before imagining the scene for ourselves through a guided meditation.

Historical Context

The scripture passage that we will enter into today is an extremely important moment in Jesus' ministry and one we commemorate every time we go to mass. The event took place in Jerusalem on the Jewish feast of the Passover (see Figure 7 - Jerusalem in the land of Israel). This is one of the three great Jewish feasts which, at the time of Jesus, saw Israelites travel to Jerusalem in order to celebrate the feast and to worship in the Temple. The Passover commemorates God's work in freeing the Israelite people from their time of exile in Egypt. The special feast was celebrated with a sacred meal of lamb, wine, herbs, and bread. This particular telling of the event comes from Mark's Gospel. This Gospel is believed to have been written by John Mark, a Jewish man who lived in Jerusalem and who was a disciple (meaning follower) of the apostle Peter.

Figure 7 - Jerusalem in the land of Israel

Let us begin this session with a prayer of petition.

In the name of the Father, the Son, and the Holy Spirit.

Holy Spirit we ask that you help guide our thoughts and our imaginations during this time of prayer, Amen.

Encounter

Use a Bible to read the passage aloud to the class. Where possible, always allow students to hold their own Bible and to read along with you.

Now sit comfortably with your Bibles open to the Gospel of Mark within the New Testament and find the large number 14 which represents Chapter 14. Now locate the small verse number 22. I will be reading Mark 14: 22-26 aloud and I ask that you silently read along with me.

Read Mark 14: 22-26 through slowly, ensuring that students are reading along

The Lord's Supper

²² While they were eating, Jesus took a piece of bread, gave a prayer of thanks, broke it, and gave it to his disciples. "Take it," he said, "this is my body." ²³ Then he took a cup, gave thanks to God, and handed it to them; and they all drank from it. ²⁴ Jesus said, "This is my blood which is poured out for many, my blood which seals God's covenant. ²⁵ I tell you, I will never again drink this wine until the day I drink the new wine in the Kingdom of God." ²⁶ Then they sang a hymn and went out to the Mount of Olives.

We are going to read it through one more time. This time as we read through, I want you to try and imagine the scene and what is happening in the story.

Read Mark 14: 22-26 slowly to the class before guiding the students through the scene

Thank you for reading along. Now that you are familiar with the story, I'd like you to close your Bibles and find a comfortable place to lay down on the floor. We're now

Eucharist

going to begin the meditation part of our prayer, where we allow the Holy Spirit to guide our imaginations. I will help to lead you through the process, asking you what it is that you can see, hear, touch, smell and even taste. Try to remain relaxed. If you get distracted, don't worry, just try and remain quiet so you don't distract others. Then re-focus back on your imagination and allow my voice to guide you. Don't worry about where your imagination takes you or whether it seems appropriate. The idea behind this form of prayer is that the Holy Spirit is leading your thoughts and guiding you through your imagination, so try to trust the Spirit and know there is no right or wrong way to do this.

Imagine

Let's begin by closing our eyes and taking in three slow deep breaths. Breathing in and out, in and out, in and out.

As you breathe in, try and imagine yourself in an upper room. Look at the walls, the roof, the floor. If it is possible reach out and gently touch the wall.

Take a moment now to look more closely at the room around you, noticing if it is dark or light. Maybe there are candles or oil lamps to brighten the room? Ahead of you, you can see a table that has been prepared for you and your friends to commemorate the Passover. Look at the meal laid out in front of you. What exactly can you see? What food, drinks or decorations are there?

Now pay attention to any sounds that you can hear. Is there music being played, or perhaps there are people talking, or even singing?

As you take in another deep breath notice what smells are filling the room. Can you name a specific smell?

Now look around the room at the other guests that are joining you this evening. How many people can you see? Do you recognise many of the guests? Can you talk to anyone?

As you take in the scene around you, you see a man smiling warmly at you. When you realise it is Jesus you smile back. He gestures for you to come over and sit next to him. You walk over towards Jesus and you greet him. After your greeting you sit down next to him and begin to enjoy the prepared meal. During the meal you notice as Jesus takes up the bread and blesses it. Can you hear his blessing? What words does he say?

You watch as he breaks the bread and then gives it, saying "Take it, this is my body." Jesus looks at you as he offers you some of the bread. You accept it and eat of it. What does it taste like? Is it as you expected?

Once everyone has eaten Jesus picks up a cup and gives thanks. Who is he thanking? What exactly does he say? He offers it to all of the guests and says "This is my blood which is poured out for many, my blood which seals God's covenant."

You watch as the cup makes its way around the table. When Jesus offers it to you, you accept. You first have a smell and then you take a sip. Can you describe it? What can you taste?

How does it feel to be sharing this meal with Jesus?

Look around at the others enjoying their meal. How are they reacting to this experience? As your eyes wander the room you hear Jesus say "I tell you, I will never again drink this wine until the day I drink the new wine in the Kingdom of God." You turn to him, trying to understand what he means by that. He looks back at you. He smiles again at you and you feel at peace. Take a moment to speak with Jesus. Feel free to share a story with him or to ask him a question, or to simply listen to what he would like to say to you. I will give you some time now to talk with Jesus.

Allow students time to talk with Jesus

When you have finished your conversation with Jesus you look around and notice that everyone has finished their meals and are getting ready to leave. You too stand up and you take a moment to say a proper goodbye to Jesus.

As you start to walk out of the room you turn back once to wave to Jesus.

The time has come now to return to this room, so when you feel you are ready, begin by gently squeezing your hands, wriggling your toes, and then slowly start to open your eyes.

As you sit your bodies back up, we will say a short prayer of thanksgiving.
We thank you Holy Spirit for guiding our imaginations today and allowing us to experience God's word in this way.
I invite you now to speak aloud any prayers that you may like to share with the group.

Allow a moment for spontaneous prayer

Now that we have finished the meditation, I ask you to please move yourselves into a circle so that we can have a discussion about what you have just experienced in your imagination.

Discuss

1. Can you describe the upper room and the Passover meal? What did you see, feel, hear, smell and taste?
2. How did you greet Jesus when you arrived and how did it make you feel?
3. What was it like eating and drinking what Jesus offered you? Did it taste as you expected?
4. In what way was your experience of the Passover meal with Jesus either similar or different to the celebration of the Eucharist at mass?
5. What did you speak to Jesus about at the end of the meal and what do you want to remember about the conversation?

Contemplate

Now to finish off we're going to take 10-15 minutes for contemplation, to really reflect upon the story of the Lord's Supper. During this time you can respond to your imaginative prayer experience in a variety of different ways.

One response could be to write a recount or a snapshot describing in detail what you saw and felt during the imaginative prayer. A different written response might be to compose a prayer or write a letter to help you remember the experience at a later time. For those of you who would prefer to draw, focus your drawing on a specific moment within the imaginative prayer experience that stood out to you in a powerful or vivid way. As you reflect, in whatever way you would like, think about the significance of this meal. Why did Jesus share this meal with his friends? Why is it important that we continue to share this meal at mass?

** Have some quiet reflective music playing in the background whilst children work**

Eucharist

Feeding of Five Thousand

Mark 6: 30-44 GNT Catholic Edition

In today's imaginative prayer we will be imagining ourselves as participants at the Feeding of the Five Thousand. We will begin by reading the passage together from the Bible before imagining the scene for ourselves through a guided meditation.

Historical Context

The feeding of the five thousand is the only miracle, apart from Jesus' resurrection, which is recorded in all four gospels. Today we will be reading Mark's account however you might like to look up the other three gospel accounts in your own time (Matthew 14:13–21, Luke 9:10–17, John 6:1–15).

In this passage we will hear about a time when thousands of people had followed Jesus in order to hear him speak. After preaching to them, Jesus realised that many in the crowd were hungry and he asked his disciples what they could do to help. We will hear that one disciple suggests going into a town to buy the crowd food, although this would not have been a realistic option because, as the scripture tells us, to do so would have cost 200 silver coins. This was a lot of money, considering just 1 silver coin was equal to a whole day's wages. This event takes place on the banks of the Sea of Galilee (see Figure 8 - The Sea of Galilee).

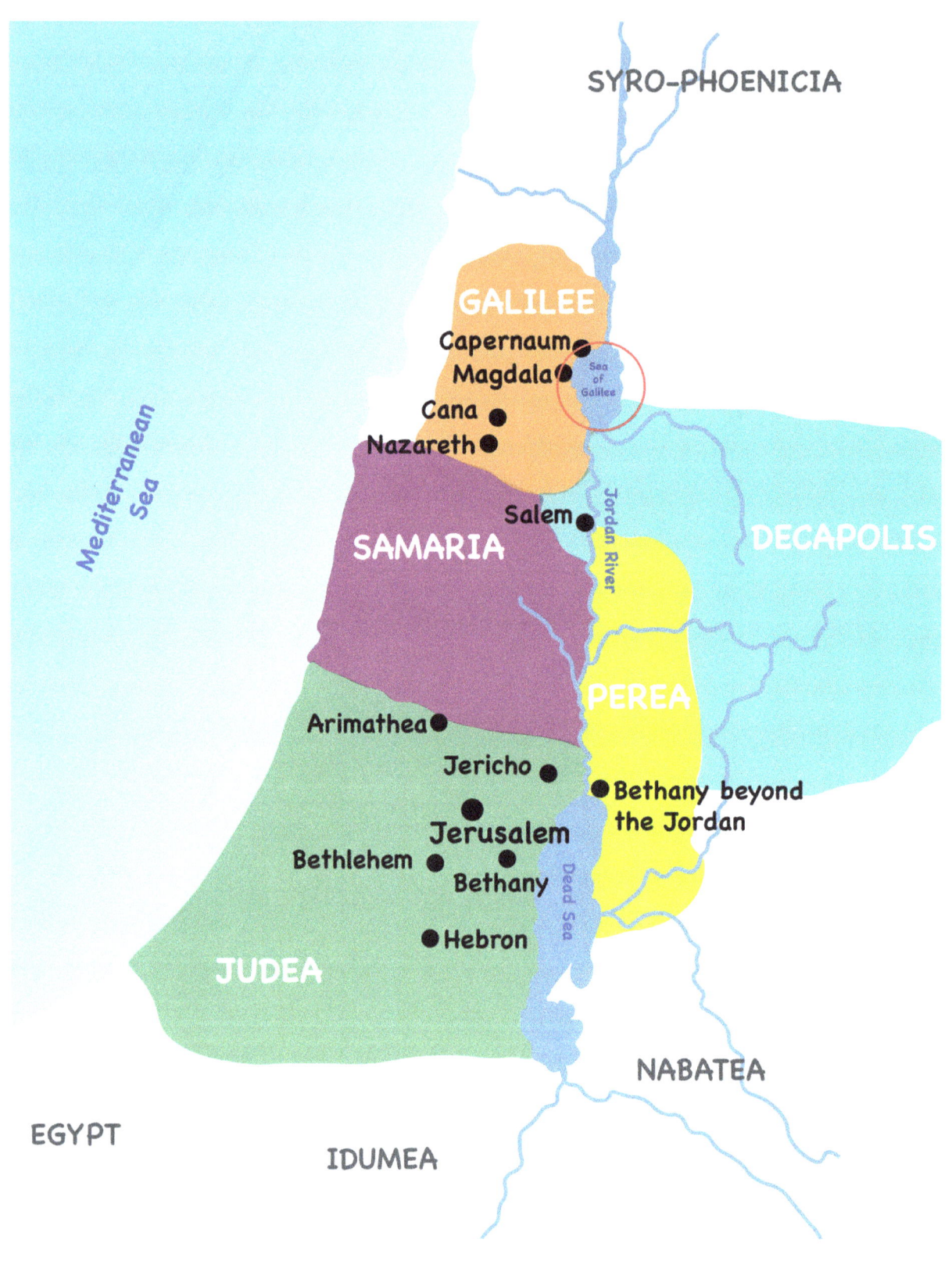

Figure 8 - The Sea of Galilee

Eucharist

Let us begin this session with a prayer of petition.

In the name of the Father, the Son, and the Holy Spirit.

Holy Spirit we ask that you help guide our thoughts and our imaginations during this time of prayer, Amen.

Encounter

Use a Bible to read the passage aloud to the class. Where possible, always allow students to hold their own Bible and to read along with you.

Now sit comfortably with your Bibles open to the Gospel of Mark within the New Testament and find the large number 6 which represents Chapter 6. Now locate the small 30 which represents verse 30. I will be reading Mark 6: 30-44 aloud and I ask that you silently read along with me.

Read Mark 6: 30-44 through slowly, ensuring that students are reading along

Jesus Feeds Five Thousand

³⁰The apostles returned and met with Jesus, and told him all they had done and taught. ³¹There were so many people coming and going that Jesus and his disciples didn't even have time to eat. So he said to them, "Let us go off by ourselves to some place where we will be alone and you can rest a while." ³²So they started out in a boat by themselves to a lonely place.

³³Many people, however, saw them leave and knew at once who they were; so they went from all the towns and ran ahead by land and arrived at the place ahead of Jesus and his disciples. ³⁴When Jesus got out of the boat, he saw this large crowd, and his heart was filled with pity for them, because they were like sheep without a shepherd. So he began to teach them many things. ³⁵When it was getting late, his disciples came to him and said, "It is already very late, and this is a lonely place. ³⁶Send the people away, and let them go to the nearby farms and villages in order to buy themselves something to eat."

³⁷"You yourselves give them something to eat," Jesus answered.

They asked, "Do you want us to go and spend two hundred silver coins on bread in order to feed them?"

³⁸So Jesus asked them, "How much bread do you have? Go and see."

When they found out, they told him, "Five loaves and also two fish."

³⁹Jesus then told his disciples to make all the people divide into groups and sit down on the green grass. ⁴⁰So the people sat down in rows, in groups of a hundred and groups of fifty. ⁴¹Then Jesus took the five loaves and the two fish, looked up to heaven, and gave thanks to God. He broke the loaves and gave them to his disciples to distribute to the people. He also divided the two fish among them all. ⁴²Everyone ate and had enough. ⁴³Then the disciples took up twelve baskets full of what was left of the bread and the fish. ⁴⁴The number of men who were fed was five thousand.

We are going to read it through one more time. This time as we read through, I want you to try and imagine the scene and what is happening in the story.

Read Mark 6: 30-44 slowly to the class before guiding the students through the scene

Thank you for reading along. Now that you are familiar with the story, I'd like you to close your Bibles and find a comfortable place to lay down on the floor. We're now going to begin the meditation part of our prayer, where we allow the Holy Spirit to guide our imaginations. I will help to lead you through the process, asking you what it is that you can see, hear, touch, smell and even taste. Try to remain relaxed. If you get distracted, don't worry, just try and remain quiet so you don't distract others. Then re-focus back on your imagination and allow my voice to guide you. Don't worry about where your imagination takes you or whether it seems appropriate. The idea behind this form of prayer is that the Holy Spirit is leading your thoughts and guiding you through your imagination, so try to trust the Spirit and know there is no right or wrong way to do this.

Eucharist

Imagine

Let's begin by closing our eyes and taking in three slow deep breaths. Breathing in and out, in and out, in and out.

As you breathe in try and imagine yourself along the banks of the Sea of Galilee, surrounded by thousands of people. The sun is starting to set and you look around, noticing the endless number of faces around you. It has been a long day, you travelled here on foot to listen to a preacher named Jesus. He has been teaching the crowd for hours.

Can you see Jesus amongst the crowd? If you can, take a moment to really notice him. What stands out to you about him? How do you know it is Jesus?

As you watch, notice if he is still speaking aloud to the crowd. If so, can you hear what he is saying?

As you are listening, you start to notice many of the people around you looking tired and hungry. Are you feeling hungry too?

You look back over and notice that Jesus has gathered a group of his disciples around him and they appear to be discussing something very intently.

Watch them as they speak to one another. How many disciples can you see around Jesus? Do they looked happy, worried or upset as they speak with him?

Suddenly the group separate and the disciples begin entering the crowd. You overhear one of the disciples asking people if they have any food they could offer.

Are they really asking the crowd for food? Who is the food going to be for? Are they asking for Jesus? What about all of these people who themselves are hungry? Perhaps you yourself have food to offer.

It is not long before the disciples return and gather around Jesus. You see that there only appears to be a tiny amount of food in their hands. You strain your eyes to see. Is that bread and fish that they are holding?

Almost immediately you see the disciples moving again, this time telling the crowd of people to organise themselves into groups of 50 or 100 and to sit in rows on the grass. You quickly get up and move to be part of a group.

But you wonder to yourself, what is going on? Why does everyone have to move?

As you move to join a row you look back over towards Jesus and notice that he is holding the food up towards the sky like an offering. Although you can see that his mouth is moving, you are unable to hear what he is saying due to the noise of the crowd. What do you notice about him?

The disciples return from organising the crowd, this time with baskets that they have collected from the people. How do the disciples seem? Do you think any of them understand what is going on?

You continue to watch Jesus and his disciples. What do you see happening? What are they doing with the baskets? What expressions do you notice on the disciples faces?

Suddenly the disciples pick up the baskets and move into the crowd, handing out bread and fish to everyone in the groups.

You yourself receive a serving of the food. Who is it that presents it to you?

Look at the food in your hand. Take in a deep breath and smell what you are holding. As the feeling of hunger takes over you begin to eat the food. Notice the taste and the texture of the food as you eat.

You continue eating, until you feel satisfied and then look around and notice the reactions of the crowd. Do you hear any talking? Or are there other sounds that stand out to you?

As you scan the mass of people, you notice the disciples beginning to collect leftover food from the crowd. You wonder how there could possibly be food leftover.

How is it that everyone has been fed? Take a moment to really think about this.

The time has come now to return to this room, so when you feel you are ready, begin by gently squeezing your hands, wriggling your toes, and then slowly start to open your eyes.

As you sit your bodies back up, we will say a short prayer of thanksgiving.

We thank you Holy Spirit for guiding our imaginations today and allowing us to experience God's word in this way.

I invite you now to speak aloud any prayers that you may like to share with the group.

Allow a moment for spontaneous prayer

Eucharist

Now that we have finished the meditation, I ask you to please move yourselves into a circle so that we can have a discussion about what you have just experienced in your imagination.

Discuss

1. Describe the scene as you were sitting and listening to Jesus on the banks of the Sea of Galilee. What did you notice with each of your senses?

2. Was there something that stood out to you about Jesus? How did you recognise that it was him?

3. Describe what occurred after the disciples brought the empty baskets to Jesus? What did you see happening with Jesus, the disciples and the baskets?

4. What was it like eating the food that was handed out by the disciples? What could you smell and taste?

5. Why do you think this event was so important in the life and mission of Jesus that all four gospel writers included it?

Contemplate

Now to finish off we're going to take 10-15 minutes for contemplation, to really reflect upon the feeding of the five thousand event. During this time you can respond to your imaginative prayer experience in a variety of different ways.

One response could be to write a recount or a snapshot describing in detail what you saw and felt during the imaginative prayer. A different written response might be to compose a prayer or write a letter to help you remember the experience at a later time. For those of you who would prefer to draw, focus your drawing on a specific moment within the imaginative prayer experience that stood out to you in a powerful or vivid way. As you reflect, in whatever way you would like, think about why this event was seen as so significant in the life of Jesus that it was recorded by all four gospel writers. Perhaps you could think about what God is trying to tell you through this event?

** Have some quiet reflective music playing in the background whilst children work**

Eucharist

Jesus the Bread of Life

John 6: 25-59 GNT Catholic Edition

In today's imaginative prayer we will be immersing ourselves into a particularly difficult scripture passage, known as the bread of life discourse. Jesus' teaching was so difficult for the listeners to understand, that many decided to get up and leave, no longer willing to follow him. We will first begin by reading the passage together from the Bible before imagining the scene for ourselves in a meditation.

Historical Context

Today's scripture passage comes from the Gospel of John. The interaction occurs not long after Jesus had fed the 5000 on the edge of the Sea of Galilee, after which many people followed Jesus and travelled across the water to Capernaum. While in Capernaum Jesus was found teaching in the Synagogue (see Figure 9 - Capernaum). A Synagogue is a place where Jews would go to hear the Jewish Scriptures read aloud. This was very important at the time because most people were unable to read or write and so the synagogue was the main way that the people could learn about God.

The crowd who had followed Jesus had been demanding more signs and miracles from him, asking him to prove himself. In the discussion they speak with Jesus about an account from the Jewish Scriptures (Old Testament) where the people of Israel were in the desert, and were fed something called 'manna'. The people of Israel had just fled from slavery in Egypt, they were isolated and without food, and yet God provided for them. The Bible tells us that the manna that God sent down from the heavens each night was like a flaky wafer and the people of Israel would collect it each morning so that everyone could eat. Often the manna that God provided was referred to as the *Bread of Heaven*. In the passage we will read, Jesus calls himself the true bread of heaven, because whoever eats of his flesh will have eternal life. This doesn't mean that people will live on earth forever, but that through Jesus and a unity with Him, people can live with him forever in the heavenly life.

The crowd in the Synagogue, which we will be a part of, becomes very confused and begins to complain because they know Jesus' mother and father, yet he is claiming that he is 'from heaven'. In responding to them Jesus does not change what he says or try and make it easier to listen to, instead he goes even further with his claim, stating "I am the bread of life [...], if you do not eat the flesh of the Son of Man and drink his blood, you will not have life in yourselves."

Just remember as we journey together today, that this is a very difficult passage of Scripture to understand, yet it is a passage that is crucial in understanding the Catholic Church's teaching on the Eucharist at Mass. If at any time you feel strange or uncomfortable hearing Jesus speak like this, just know that it was just as difficult for the disciples who knew and followed Jesus when he was alive on Earth, with many choosing to stop following him after hearing this teaching.

Figure 9 - Capernaum

Let us begin this session with a prayer of petition.

In the name of the Father, the Son, and the Holy Spirit.

Holy Spirit we ask that you help guide our thoughts and our imaginations during this time of prayer, Amen.

Encounter

Use a Bible to read the passage aloud to the class. Where possible, always allow students to hold their own Bible and to read along with you.

Now sit comfortably with your Bibles open to the Gospel of John within the New Testament and find the large number 6 which represents Chapter 6. Now locate the small number 48, this is called the verse. I will be slowly reading John 6: 48-59 aloud to you and I ask that you silently read along with me.

Read John 6: 48-59 through slowly, ensuring that students are reading along

Jesus the Bread of Life

⁴⁸ I am the bread of life. ⁴⁹ Your ancestors ate manna in the desert, but they died. ⁵⁰But the bread that comes down from heaven is of such a kind that whoever eats it will not die. ⁵¹ I am the living bread that came down from heaven. If you eat this bread, you will live forever. The bread that I will give you is my flesh, which I give so that the world may live."

⁵² This started an angry argument among them. "How can this man give us his flesh to eat?" they asked.

⁵³ Jesus said to them, "I am telling you the truth: if you do not eat the flesh of the Son of Man and drink his blood, you will not have life in yourselves. ⁵⁴ Those who eat my flesh and drink my blood have eternal life, and I will raise them to life on the last day. ⁵⁵ For my flesh is the real food; my blood is the real drink. ⁵⁶ Those who eat my flesh and drink my blood live in me, and I live in them. ⁵⁷ The living Father sent me, and because of him I live also. In the same way whoever eats me will live because of me. ⁵⁸ This, then, is the bread that came

Eucharist

down from heaven; it is not like the bread that your ancestors ate, but then later died. Those who eat this bread will live forever."
⁵⁹ Jesus said this as he taught in the synagogue in Capernaum.

We are going to read it through one more time. This time as we read through, I want you to try and imagine the scene and what is happening in the story.

Read John 6: 48-59 slowly to the class before guiding the students through the scene

Thank you for reading along. Now that you are familiar with the story, I'd like you to close your Bibles and find a comfortable place to lay down on the floor. We're now going to begin the meditation part of our prayer, where we allow the Holy Spirit to guide our imaginations. I will help to lead you through the process, asking you what it is that you can see, hear, touch, smell and even taste. Try to remain relaxed. If you get distracted, don't worry, just try and remain quiet so you don't distract others. Then re-focus back on your imagination and allow my voice to guide you. Don't worry about where your imagination takes you or whether it seems appropriate. The idea behind this form of prayer is that the Holy Spirit is leading your thoughts and guiding you through your imagination, so try to trust the Spirit and know there is no right or wrong way to do this.

Imagine

Let's begin by closing our eyes and taking in three slow deep breaths. Breathing in and out, in and out, in and out.

As you breathe in try and imagine yourself sitting down inside the rectangular-shaped room of the Synagogue. Take a moment to notice what stands out to you about the room. Perhaps you can see some tiered stone benches lining the walls of the room.

As you look around, notice if there is any sunlight coming into the space. Notice if it feels warm or cold inside the room?

Now take a moment and really listen to what sounds you can hear. Perhaps there are also certain smells that you notice?

As you explore the room with your eyes, pay attention to what else you can see. For instance, how many people are there in the synagogue and do you recognise anyone that is around you?

Can you see Jesus? If so, what do you notice about him? Can he also see you?

As you continue looking around the room you begin to notice the discomfort and unease of the people around you. Many are starting to grumble about some of the things that Jesus has already said, especially the words "I am the bread of life."

Jesus has already compared himself to the manna which our Jewish ancestors had been given by God to eat in the desert and many in the crowd now seem confused and unsure about what Jesus is saying. Some are murmuring quietly and asking others how this man, the son of Joseph and Mary, could possibly claim to be the 'bread that will sustain us'? It doesn't help that many of the people here have given up their lives to follow Jesus, and now they don't even understand what he is saying.

In amongst the muttering, you look around and see that Jesus is standing in the middle of the room, and you watch him closely, noticing his expression and hand gestures, as he begins speaking to the unsettled crowd.

> "I am the living bread that came down from heaven. If you eat this bread, you will live forever. The bread that I will give you is my flesh, which I give so that the world may live."

You feel the change in energy of the room as the tension seems to grow amongst the people, many becoming angry by Jesus' words. You hear a man call out from the other side of the room "How can this man give us his flesh to eat?"

Jesus turns toward the man, whilst still speaking to all who are gathered,

> "I am telling you the truth: if you do not eat the flesh of the Son of Man and drink his blood, you will not have life in yourselves. Those who eat my flesh and drink my blood have eternal life, and I will raise them to life on the last day."

Questions start running through your mind……Eat of his flesh and drink of his blood? But surely he is not asking us to really do that. We cannot possibly eat the flesh of a human person. We can't even eat of an animal unless the blood has first been drained, for blood is considered a sign of life. What can he possibly be asking of us?

While all of these questions are running through your mind, you turn to see the faces of those around you. How are people feeling as they listen to these words?

Look back towards Jesus, what is the expression on his face?

What is he really telling you right now? What does he really mean by all of this?

As you struggle to make sense of Jesus' words, you hear him continue to speak.

"My flesh is the real food" Jesus proclaims, "my blood is the real drink. Those who eat my flesh and drink my blood live in me, and I live in them."

How can Jesus *live* in me, when he is standing right there? What does that even mean?

Will there come a time when Jesus won't be here in the Synagogue with us?

Is that what he is speaking about?

Jesus finishes by saying "The living Father sent me, and because of him I live also. In the same way whoever eats me will live because of me."

The Father sent him? Does he mean the God of Israel has sent him? The God who sent our ancestors manna in the desert?

You watch as people begin to turn and walk out of the Synagogue, noticeably upset. Jesus' twelve close disciples stay near him but many others choose to leave.

How are *you* feeling in this moment? Do you also feel like you should leave?

Look over at Jesus and notice the expression on his face. How do you think He is feeling as he watches many of his followers leave?

After a moment he sees you watching him and he comes toward you. How are you feeling now, with Jesus right there in front of you.

Is there something you would like to ask him? Is there something on your heart that you would like to share with him? Take a moment now to speak with Jesus.

Allow students time to talk with Jesus

Now that you have had some time alone to speak with Jesus it's time to say a proper goodbye. As you begin to walk out of the room you think once more about those strange words that Jesus had shared with the crowd, to eat his flesh and drink his blood.

The time has come to return to this room, so when you feel you are ready, begin by gently squeezing your hands, wriggling your toes, and then slowly start to open your eyes.

As you sit your bodies back up, we will say a short prayer of thanksgiving.
We thank you Holy Spirit for guiding our imaginations today and allowing us to experience God's word in this way.
I invite you now to speak aloud any prayers that you may like to share with the group.

Allow a moment for spontaneous prayer

Now that we have finished the meditation, I ask you to please move yourselves into a circle so that we can have a discussion about what you have just experienced in your imagination.

Discuss

1. Can you describe the Synagogue? What could you see, feel, hear and smell?

2. What did you notice about Jesus' tone and expressions as he spoke to the crowd? How do you think he was feeling?

3. How did *you* feel when many people decided to walk out? How do you think Jesus felt when he saw the crowd respond in that way?

4. How do the words of Jesus in this passage help us to understand the Eucharist at Mass?

Eucharist

5. Did you take the opportunity to speak directly with Jesus, and if so, what is the message or memory you want to take away from that conversation?

Contemplate

Now to finish off we're going to take 10-15 minutes for contemplation. This will allow you time to really reflect upon this difficult passage, known as 'The Bread of Life Discourse'. During this time you can respond to your imaginative prayer experience in a variety of different ways.

One response could be to write a recount or a snapshot describing in detail what you saw and felt during the imaginative prayer. A different written response might be to compose a prayer or write a letter to help you remember the experience at a later time. For those of you who would prefer to draw, focus your drawing on a specific moment within the imaginative prayer experience that stood out to you in a powerful or vivid way. As you reflect, in whatever way you would like, think about Jesus' words to his followers. How might this relate to the celebration of the Eucharist at Holy Mass? What message do you think Jesus might be trying to share with you through this passage?

** Have some quiet reflective music playing in the background whilst children work**

The Walk to Emmaus

Luke 24: 13-33 GNT Catholic Edition

In today's imaginative prayer we will be imagining ourselves as participants walking along a dirt road on our way from Jerusalem to a town called Emmaus. We will begin by reading the passage together from the Bible before imagining the scene for ourselves through a guided meditation.

Historical Context

The story of the walk to Emmaus is only told in the Gospel of Luke. It takes place after Jesus' death on the cross outside of the city of Jerusalem, and as we will hear in the passage, it is also after the women had gone to visit Jesus' tomb and found it to be empty.

The two people who are walking on the road to the town of Emmaus are at first unable to recognise Jesus who joins them on their journey. The author of Luke's Gospel, tells us that the distance between Jerusalem and Emmaus was 7 miles, or just over 11km. To travel this distance could have taken between 2 and 3 hours of walking (see Figure 10 - Jerusalem to Emmaus).

The structure of this walk to Emmaus account is very similar to the structure of the Holy Mass. It begins with the sharing of the words of scripture, it continued with the breaking of bread, and it ends with the two friends being sent out to share their experience of faith with others.

Figure 10 - Jerusalem to Emmaus

Let us begin this session with a prayer of petition.

In the name of the Father, the Son, and the Holy Spirit.

Holy Spirit we ask that you help guide our thoughts and our imaginations during this time of prayer, Amen.

Encounter

Use a Bible to read the passage aloud to the class. Where possible, always allow students to hold their own Bible and to read along with you.

Now sit comfortably with your Bibles open to the Gospel of Luke within the New Testament and find the large number 24 which represents Chapter 24. Now locate the small 13 which represents verse 13. I will be reading Luke 24: 13-33 aloud and I ask that you silently read along with me.

Read Luke 24: 13-33 through slowly, ensuring that students are reading along

The Walk to Emmaus

13 On that same day two of Jesus' followers were going to a village named Emmaus, about seven miles from Jerusalem, 14 and they were talking to each other about all the things that had happened. 15 As they talked and discussed, Jesus himself drew near and walked along with them; 16 they saw him, but somehow did not recognize him. 17 Jesus said to them, "What are you talking about to each other, as you walk along?"

They stood still, with sad faces. 18 One of them, named Cleopas, asked him, "Are you the only visitor in Jerusalem who doesn't know the things that have been happening there these last few days?"

19 "What things?" he asked.

"The things that happened to Jesus of Nazareth," they answered. "This man was a prophet and was considered by God and by all the people to be powerful in everything he said and did. 20 Our chief priests and rulers handed him over to be sentenced to death, and he was crucified. 21 And we had hoped that he would be the one who was going to set Israel free!

Eucharist

Besides all that, this is now the third day since it happened. [22] *Some of the women of our group surprised us; they went at dawn to the tomb,* [23] *but could not find his body. They came back saying they had seen a vision of angels who told them that he is alive.* [24] *Some of our group went to the tomb and found it exactly as the women had said, but they did not see him."*

[25] *Then Jesus said to them, "How foolish you are, how slow you are to believe everything the prophets said!* [26] *Was it not necessary for the Messiah to suffer these things and then to enter his glory?"* [27] *And Jesus explained to them what was said about himself in all the Scriptures, beginning with the books of Moses and the writings of all the prophets.*

[28] *As they came near the village to which they were going, Jesus acted as if he were going farther;* [29] *but they held him back, saying, "Stay with us; the day is almost over and it is getting dark." So he went in to stay with them.* [30] *He sat down to eat with them, took the bread, and said the blessing; then he broke the bread and gave it to them.* [31] *Then their eyes were opened and they recognized him, but he disappeared from their sight.* [32] *They said to each other, "Wasn't it like a fire burning in us when he talked to us on the road and explained the Scriptures to us?"*

[33] *They got up at once and went back to Jerusalem, where they found the eleven disciples gathered together with the others.*

We are going to read it through one more time. This time as we read through, I want you to try and imagine the scene and what is happening in the story.

Read Luke 24: 13-33 slowly to the class before guiding the students through the scene

Thank you for reading along. Now that you are familiar with the story, I'd like you to close your Bibles and find a comfortable place to lay down on the floor. We're now going to begin the meditation part of our prayer, where we allow the Holy Spirit to guide our imaginations. I will help to lead you through the process, asking you what it is that you can see, hear, touch, smell and even taste. Try to remain relaxed. If you get distracted, don't worry, just try and remain quiet so you don't distract others. Then re-focus back on your imagination and allow my voice to guide you. Don't worry about where your imagination takes you or whether it seems appropriate. The idea behind this form of prayer is that the Holy Spirit is leading your thoughts and guiding you through your imagination, so try to trust the Spirit and know that there is no right or wrong way to do this.

Imagine

Let's begin by closing our eyes and taking in three slow deep breaths. Breathing in and out, in and out, in and out.

As you breathe in try and imagine yourself walking along a dirt road. You and a friend have left Jerusalem and are making your way to the town of Emmaus. Look around you, what is the weather like? Are there many other people travelling along the road? What does the road feel like under foot?

Take in a deep breath, noticing if there are any distinct smells as you journey along. Pay attention to any sounds that you can hear, such as other people talking or animals in the distance.

As you walk along you think about all that has taken place over the last three days in Jerusalem, after the death of Jesus. Notice how you are feeling as you walk along beside your friend. How are you feeling now that Jesus is no longer with you and the disciples? You spend the journey talking with your friend about all that you are feeling.

It is not long before another man comes closer to you and joins in with your conversation, asking "What are you talking about to each other, as you walk along?"

You take in a deep breath and wonder how to respond to such a question. How can this man not know what we would be talking about, everyone in Jerusalem has been talking about it. Your friend answers him, "Are you the only visitor in Jerusalem who doesn't know the things that have been happening there these last few days?"

Notice the tone of the man's words as he responds by saying "What things?"

Your friend begins to explain all that has happened to Jesus of Nazareth, the powerful prophet who had been handed over to be crucified by the Chief Priests and rulers. You listen as your friend retells the story of the women who came to you and the disciples after visiting the tomb and finding it empty.

Eucharist

You continue to watch on as your friend explains "Some of our group went to the tomb and found it exactly as the women had said, but they did not see him."

The man that has just joined you then responds by saying "How foolish are you, how slow you are to believe everything the prophets said! Was it not necessary for the Messiah to suffer these things and then to enter his glory?"

Take a breath. Who is this person? What is he saying? Have you been a fool? What does it even mean when he says that the Messiah had to suffer?

Notice how you are feeling right now? Do you want to keep walking along with this man and your friend? You look around and as you think about what you should do, the man continues to speak. You listen as he shares the story of God's plan for salvation with you, beginning with the stories you know from the books of Moses and then he continues by sharing insights from the writings of the prophets.

What is it like hearing the Scriptures being shared in this way?

Take a moment to really listen to what this man has to say.

Allow students time to really listen to Jesus

As you all come nearer to the village, you and your friend begin to walk towards the houses, however the man with you continues to walk along the road.

Your friend calls out to him saying, "Stay with us, the day is almost over and it is getting dark."

You watch the man carefully as you all walk together into the house where you plan to stay the night. As you enter the house, and make your way to the table, take a moment to look around. Is it dark inside or are there candles or lanterns to brighten the room? Notice the smell of the room and any sounds you can hear as you sit yourself down at the table.

Your friend brings the food to the table, and you wait for your friend to break the bread to signify the start of the meal. However, instead of your friend, it is your guest, the man who joined you, who picks up the bread, says the blessings and then breaks it.

As he hands it to you, suddenly everything seems to change. You look at the man and you recognise who he is! Jesus, the one who had died and has now risen!

How is it possible? How did you not know that it was him?

You look at your friend who seems amazed. As you turn back though, Jesus has gone, he is no longer sitting with you at the table.

How did he leave? Why did he go?

Take another breath and allow yourself to think about what just happened. How are you feeling right now? Are you shocked, confused, overjoyed?

With so many thoughts running through your head, your friend looks at you and says "Wasn't it like a fire burning in us when he talked to us on the road and explained the Scriptures to us?"

You take in another breath. So many questions are going through your mind. Allow the Holy Spirit time to answer them.

The time has come to return to this room, so when you feel you are ready, begin by gently squeezing your hands, wriggling your toes, and then slowly start to open your eyes.

As you sit your bodies back up, we will say a short prayer of thanksgiving.

We thank you Holy Spirit for guiding our imaginations today and allowing us to experience God's word in this way.

I invite you now to speak aloud any prayers that you may like to share with the group.

Allow a moment for spontaneous prayer

Now that we have finished the meditation, I ask you to please move yourselves into a circle so that we can have a discussion about what you have just experienced in your imagination.

1. Can you describe what you noticed with each of your senses as you were walking along the road? How were you feeling?

Eucharist

2. What did you notice about the man who joined you on the journey? What stood out to you about him?

3. What were some of the things that the man spoke to you about as you journeyed along?

4. Describe the room where you sat down to share the meal, what could you see, feel, touch and smell?

5. Explain how you felt in that moment when you recognised that it was Jesus eating with you, and then how you felt when he suddenly disappeared?

6. What can we learn from this experience that can help us to better understand the Holy Mass?

Contemplate

Now to finish off we're going to take 10-15 minutes for contemplation, to really reflect upon the journey to Emmaus and the meal. During this time you can respond to your imaginative prayer experience in a variety of different ways.

One response could be to write a recount or a snapshot describing in detail what you saw and felt during the imaginative prayer. A different written response might be to compose a prayer or write a letter to help you remember the experience at a later time. For those of you who would prefer to draw, focus your drawing on a specific moment within the imaginative prayer experience that stood out to you in a powerful or vivid way. As you reflect, in whatever way you would like, think about why the author of Luke's Gospel chose to include this particular encounter in his gospel. Perhaps you could also think about what God might be trying to tell you through this story?

** Have some quiet reflective music playing in the background whilst children work**

Reconciliation

Introduction to the Sacrament of Penance and Reconciliation

Throughout his earthly ministry, Jesus' preaching centred on God's mercy, love, and forgiveness. After his resurrection, he commissioned his apostles to continue his ministry so that the Good News of salvation would be known throughout the world. He told them, "if you forgive the sins of any they are forgiven, if you retain the sins of any, they are retained" (John 20:23). In doing so Jesus instituted the Sacrament of Penance and Reconciliation.

The Sacrament of Penance and Reconciliation provides us with an opportunity to acknowledge our sinfulness and receive God's mercy and forgiveness. Sin, simply understood, is a deliberate act which harms our relationship with God. If we understand God's expectations for us yet we knowingly behave in a way that is contrary to that, then we inevitably hurt ourselves, others, or God. Examples of such sins could include showing road rage, talking about people behind their backs, or even choosing not to go to Mass on a Holy Day of Obligation (e.g. a Sunday) due to a desire to sleep in.

Most sins are the result of small actions and decisions that we assume will not affect anyone else. Often we don't immediately see a consequence and so we continue to repeat our behaviours over and over again. Each time, any sense of guilt that we may have initially felt decreases and the actions and behaviours become even easier to repeat. God recognises that we need his help to return to the path of righteousness, and it is for this reason that he gifted us the Sacrament of Penance and Reconciliation. The sacrament allows us to acknowledge the times when we have sinned, to ask for God's mercy and forgiveness, and to receive the strength from God's grace that we need in order to not sin again. This ongoing conversion and reestablishment of our relationship with the Lord is necessary for a life of faith.

The Sacrament of Penance and Reconciliation is sometimes referred to by other names, such as the Sacrament of Confession, the Sacrament of Forgiveness, or the Sacrament of Conversion. There are four distinct but related parts to the sacramental celebration:

1. **Contrition:** refers to the feeling of sorrow experienced when you realise that you have acted wrongly towards yourself, others, or God. This sorrow is accompanied by a desire to repent, to make amends, and to turn away from such behaviours.

2. **Confession:** is the time to be open and honest with God about the times when you know you have behaved against his will. This involves confronting your sins and speaking them aloud to a priest. Within the sacrament the priest is acting *in persona Christi*, as a representative of Christ.

3. **Penance:** is an important part of our healing which comes from completing the tasks that the priest suggests for us. The 'penance' is designed to help you acknowledge the hurt you may have caused through your actions and assists you to make amends.

4. **Absolution**: The words spoken by the priest absolve you of your sins and provides reconciliation with God and the believing community. To be reconciled means that the relationship is returned to its original state, no longer affected by the confessed sinful actions. It is as though the slate has been wiped clean.

The story of *Jesus and Zacchaeus* (p.100) is a great way to explore these different stages of the sacrament. We recognise, through the words and actions of Zacchaeus, a true conversion of heart. We can experience his desire to be united with Jesus, a desire for repentance and a true willingness to make amends for his wrongdoings. The words "salvation has come to this house today" expresses the forgiveness shown to Zacchaeus by Jesus.

Jesus at the home of Simon the Pharisee (p.107) gives us an insight into the love Jesus has for each individual person. Simon, who did not follow Jewish custom when welcoming Jesus into his home, is appalled by the doting behaviour of the intruding woman. However, Jesus uses the love shown by the woman as an example to Simon of what true faith in the Lord really is. The visible remorse that she shows through her actions

Reconciliation

are enough to communicate her desire for repentance and Jesus responds by absolving her of her sins.

The final two imaginative prayer experiences in this chapter explore the parable of the *Lost Son*, the story commonly referred to as the prodigal son. These two experiences should be completed in sequence and as part of a wider exploration of the lost parables (see p.114). The parable of the *Lost Son* has been divided into two experiences in order to focus attention on the father's individual relationship with each of his two sons (see p.117 and p.124). In separating the parable into these two imaginative prayers, students will have more time to unpack the complexity of Jesus' teaching for themselves.

Jesus and Zacchaeus

Luke 19: 1-10 GNT Catholic Edition

In today's imaginative prayer we will be imagining the story of Jesus meeting Zacchaeus. We will first begin by reading the passage together from the Bible before imagining the scene for ourselves in a meditation.

Historical Context

Today's scripture passage, known as the story of Zacchaeus, can only be found in the Gospel of Luke. It is believed that Luke wrote his gospel for a Gentile audience, meaning people who were not Jewish. Many of the stories in Luke's gospel show Jesus extending his love and forgiveness upon those who were disliked or excluded from Jewish society. This story is no different. We will hear about a short man who was so desperate to catch a glimpse of Jesus as he passed by that he decided to climb up a tree.

Zacchaeus was not a well-liked man because he worked as the chief tax collector for the region of Jericho where he lived (see Figure 11 - The town of Jericho). During this time in history the Romans were rulers of the land of Israel, ruling through violence and oppression. Despite their harsh treatment of the Jewish people, the Jews were required to pay taxes to the Romans and this money was collected by tax collectors like Zacchaeus. Not only were they disliked because they worked for the Romans, but tax collectors were also known for taking more money than they should and keeping the extra for themselves, essentially stealing from the people.

Reconciliation

Figure 11 - The town of Jericho

Let us begin this session with a prayer of petition.

In the name of the Father, the Son, and the Holy Spirit.

Holy Spirit we ask that you help guide our thoughts and our imaginations during this time of prayer, Amen.

Encounter

Use a Bible to read the passage aloud to the class. Where possible, always allow students to hold their own Bible and to read along with you.

Now sit comfortably with your Bibles open to the Gospel of Luke within the New Testament and find the large number 19 which represents Chapter 19. I will be reading Luke 19: 1-10 aloud and I ask that you silently read along with me.

Read Luke 19: 1-10 through slowly, ensuring that students are reading along

Jesus and Zacchaeus

19 Jesus went on into Jericho and was passing through. [2] There was a chief tax collector there named Zacchaeus, who was rich. [3] He was trying to see who Jesus was, but he was a little man and could not see Jesus because of the crowd. [4] So he ran ahead of the crowd and climbed a sycamore tree to see Jesus, who was going to pass that way. [5] When Jesus came to that place, he looked up and said to Zacchaeus, "Hurry down, Zacchaeus, because I must stay in your house today." [6] Zacchaeus hurried down and welcomed him with great joy. [7] All the people who saw it started grumbling, "This man has gone as a guest to the home of a sinner!" [8] Zacchaeus stood up and said to the Lord, "Listen, sir! I will give half my belongings to the poor, and if I have cheated anyone, I will pay back four times as much." [9] Jesus said to him, "Salvation has come to this house today, for this man, also, is a descendant of Abraham. [10] The Son of Man came to seek and to save the lost."

We are going to read it through one more time. This time as we read through, I want you to try and imagine the scene and what is happening in the story.

Read Luke 19: 1-10 slowly to the class before guiding the students through the scene

Reconciliation

Thank you for reading along. Now that you are familiar with the story, I'd like you to close your Bibles and find a comfortable place to lay down on the floor. We're now going to begin the meditation part of our prayer, where we allow the Holy Spirit to guide our imaginations. I will help to lead you through the process, asking you what it is that you can see, hear, touch, smell and even taste. Try to remain relaxed. If you get distracted, don't worry, just try and remain quiet so you don't distract others. Then refocus back on your imagination and allow my voice to guide you. Don't worry about where your imagination takes you or whether it seems appropriate. The idea behind this form of prayer is that the Holy Spirit is leading your thoughts and guiding you through your imagination, so try to trust the Spirit and know there is no right or wrong way to do this.

Imagine

Let's begin by closing our eyes and taking in three slow deep breaths. Breathing in and out, in and out, in and out.

As you breathe in try and imagine the scene. A crowd has gathered along the road because they have heard that Jesus of Nazareth will soon be walking through the town of Jericho on his way to Jerusalem. The people of Jericho are excited. Jesus has already performed several miracles since his arrival in town. Look around you. Where are you amongst the crowd?

Can you see people of all different ages, or is everyone a similar age to you? Take a moment to notice the weather, is the sun shining or is the sky filled with clouds?

Are there any sounds that you notice, or any distinct smells?

As you take in your surroundings you begin to notice the people becoming more and more excited. You notice people trying to stretch their bodies higher and higher in order to get a better look. You realise that Jesus must be coming. As you yourself try to see, you notice out of the corner of your eye a man climbing up a nearby sycamore tree. You instantly recognise the man as Zacchaeus, the town's chief tax collector. He is a short man and because of his job he is not well liked by the Jewish people. What do you notice about him? How is he dressed?

For a moment you find yourself distracted by him, but then you catch a glimpse of Jesus. You turn to get a better look. What do you notice about Jesus? Can you see him clearly? Notice whether he is walking alone or with other people? Are any of his disciples with him?

Is he talking to anyone? If so, what is he saying?

Pay attention to the reaction of the crowd as he walks by. Does he interact with the people gathered?

As you continue to watch, you notice Jesus stop at the base of the sycamore tree and look up toward Zacchaeus. You watch as they look at each other for a moment. What do you notice about their facial expressions? How do you think they are feeling right now?

Despite the noise of the crowd, you manage to hear Jesus say "Hurry down, Zacchaeus, because I must stay in your house today." As Jesus says this, notice the tax collector's face. Does he seem worried, amazed, or perhaps excited that Jesus wants to go to his house?

You watch as Zacchaeus quickly gets himself down from the tree. What does he say or do to greet Jesus?

You continue to watch as the two men begin walking together. Is anyone else walking along with them?

As you follow behind the men, you start to hear people from the crowd making comments, "This man has gone as a guest to the home of a sinner."

How are you feeling about this situation? Considering all of the people that were gathered, why do you think Jesus decided to go with Zacchaeus?

You continue to watch as they approach a house. You can hear Zacchaeus speaking to Jesus. You notice the tone in his voice as he says "Listen, sir! I will give half my belongings to the poor, and if I have cheated anyone, I will pay back four times as much."

How do you think Zacchaeus is feeling now? Does it seem like he is trying to apologise to Jesus or instead trying to explain himself?

What do you think about Zacchaeus' words, do you believe him when he says that he will pay back those he has cheated? Why or why not? Why do *you* think he is saying these things to Jesus?

Reconciliation

Take a moment to look at Jesus. Notice his facial expression as he talks with Zacchaeus. Does he seem happy or disappointed?

Jesus begins to speak, "Salvation has come to this house today, for this man, also, is a descendant of Abraham. The Son of Man came to seek and to save the lost."

Who is Jesus speaking to? Who was he looking at as he said those words? Was he speaking directly to Zacchaeus, to you, or to other people around you?

Spend some time now thinking about Jesus' words. The Son of Man came to seek the lost and to save them. Who might the lost be? Is it just Zacchaeus, or are there others that are lost? Are there times when *you* have been lost? Has Jesus come to seek *you*?

Take a moment to remain in the scene. As you take one final look around at the people, the buildings and the roads, are there any sounds that you notice? Can you still see a crowd gathered or have people drifted off and returned to their daily activities?

Before you leave take in one last deep breath, noticing any smells in the air.

The time has come to return to this room, so when you feel you are ready, begin by gently squeezing your hands, wriggling your toes, and then slowly start to open your eyes.

As you sit your bodies back up, we will say a short prayer of thanksgiving.

We thank you Holy Spirit for guiding our imaginations today and allowing us to experience God's word in this way.

I invite you now to speak aloud any prayers that you may like to share with the group.

Allow a moment for spontaneous prayer

Now that we have finished the meditation, I ask you to please move yourselves into a circle so that we can have a discussion about what you have just experienced in your imagination.

Discuss

1. Describe the scene as you waited amongst the crowd for Jesus. What did you see, hear, feel and smell?
2. What did you notice about Jesus when you first caught a glimpse of him?
3. How did Zacchaeus react to Jesus speaking to him in the tree? How did he greet Jesus?
4. How do you think Zacchaeus was feeling when he told Jesus that he would pay back anyone he had cheated? How did Jesus respond?
5. Do you think Zacchaeus was "lost" before he encountered Jesus? How might we be like Zacchaeus?

Contemplate

Now to finish off we're going to take 10-15 minutes for contemplation, to really reflect upon Zacchaeus' encounter with Jesus. During this time you can respond to your imaginative prayer experience in a variety of different ways.

One response could be to write a recount or a snapshot describing in detail what you saw and felt during the imaginative prayer. A different written response might be to compose a prayer or write a letter to help you remember the experience at a later time. For those of you who would prefer to draw, focus your drawing on a specific moment within the imaginative prayer experience that stood out to you in a powerful or vivid way. As you reflect, in whatever way you would like, think about Zacchaeus' conversion story and how his relationship with God was reconciled through his encounter with Jesus.

** Have some quiet reflective music playing in the background whilst children work**

Reconciliation

Jesus at the home of Simon the Pharisee

Luke 7: 36-50 GNT Catholic Edition

In today's imaginative prayer we will be imagining a time when Jesus ate a meal with a man named Simon, who was a Pharisee. The Pharisees were a group of religious Jews who were very strict in following all Jewish laws and customs, especially when it came to cleanliness and avoiding all sin. In this account Jesus forgives a woman who the Pharisee would have thought was unforgiveable.

Historical Context

Today's scripture comes from the Gospel of Luke. Like many of Luke's accounts, this story sees Jesus forgiving a woman who would have been excluded from Jewish society. Luke told many stories of Jesus showing inclusion to those who had been excluded from Jewish life, because he understood that these events in Jesus' life would have been very important for his Gentile (non-Jewish) audience.

In this account we will hear about an alabaster jar of perfume which the woman brings to meet Jesus. Alabaster was an expensive stone and the perfume inside would normally only have been used for very special occasions. This tells us that the woman is extremely generous because she doesn't just use a small amount but instead *pours* the perfume on Jesus' feet.

We also need to understand that it was Jewish custom when arriving at a house, and before sharing a meal, that a servant would first wash a visitor's feet (because they would be dirty from wearing sandals on dirt roads). After this the host would welcome a guest with a kiss on the forehead. The last action, to anoint a person on the head with oil, was only done as a way of honouring a particular guest. As we will soon read, Simon did not think it necessary to anoint Jesus, yet the woman who comes to worship him goes far beyond this gesture and instead anoints Jesus' feet.

The last thing for us to understand before we read is the saying 'to forgive someone's debt' This means that a person is no longer required to pay back the money that they owe to another person. Therefore, the person who lent the money has 'forgiven the debt' and agreed that it no longer needs to be paid back.

Let us begin this session with a prayer of petition.
In the name of the Father, the Son, and the Holy Spirit.
Holy Spirit we ask that you help guide our thoughts and our imaginations during this time of prayer, Amen.

Encounter

Use a Bible to read the passage aloud to the class. Where possible, always allow students to hold their own Bible and to read along with you.

Now sit comfortably with your Bibles open to the Gospel of Luke within the New Testament and find the large number 7 which represents Chapter 7. Then look for the small number 36, which is called the verse. I will be reading Luke 7: 36-50 aloud and I ask that you silently read along with me.

Read Luke 7: 36-50 through slowly, ensuring that students are reading along

Jesus at the Home of Simon the Pharisee
^{36}A Pharisee invited Jesus to have dinner with him, and Jesus went to his house and sat down to eat. ^{37}In that town was a woman who lived a sinful life. She heard that Jesus was eating in the Pharisee's house, so she brought an alabaster jar full of perfume ^{38}and stood behind Jesus, by his feet, crying and wetting his feet with her tears. Then she dried his feet with her hair, kissed them, and poured the perfume on them. ^{39}When the Pharisee saw this,

Reconciliation

he said to himself, "If this man really were a prophet, he would know who this woman is who is touching him; he would know what kind of sinful life she lives!"

⁴⁰Jesus spoke up and said to him, "Simon, I have something to tell you."

"Yes, Teacher," he said, "tell me."

⁴¹"There were two men who owed money to a moneylender," Jesus began. "One owed him five hundred silver coins, and the other owed him fifty. ⁴²Neither of them could pay him back, so he cancelled the debts of both. Which one, then, will love him more?"

⁴³"I suppose," answered Simon, "that it would be the one who was forgiven more."

"You are right," said Jesus. ⁴⁴Then he turned to the woman and said to Simon, "Do you see this woman? I came into your home, and you gave me no water for my feet, but she has washed my feet with her tears and dried them with her hair. ⁴⁵You did not welcome me with a kiss, but she has not stopped kissing my feet since I came. ⁴⁶You provided no olive oil for my head, but she has covered my feet with perfume. ⁴⁷I tell you, then, the great love she has shown proves that her many sins have been forgiven. But whoever has been forgiven little shows only a little love."

⁴⁸Then Jesus said to the woman, "Your sins are forgiven."

⁴⁹The others sitting at the table began to say to themselves, "Who is this, who even forgives sins?"

⁵⁰But Jesus said to the woman, "Your faith has saved you; go in peace."

We are going to read it through one more time. This time as we read through, I want you to try and imagine the scene and what is happening in the story.

Read Luke 7: 36-50 slowly to the class before guiding the students through the scene

Thank you for reading along. Now that you are familiar with the story, I'd like you to close your Bibles and find a comfortable place to lay down on the floor. We're now going to begin the meditation part of our prayer, where we allow the Holy Spirit to guide our imaginations. I will help to lead you through the process, asking you what it is that you can see, hear, touch, smell and even taste. Try to remain relaxed. If you get distracted, don't worry, just try and remain quiet so you don't distract others. Then re-focus back on your imagination and allow my voice to guide you. Don't worry about where your imagination takes you or whether it seems appropriate. The idea behind this form of prayer is that the Holy Spirit is leading your thoughts and guiding you through your imagination, so try to trust the Spirit and know there is no right or wrong way to do this.

Imagine

Let's begin by closing our eyes and taking in three slow deep breaths. Breathing in and out, in and out, in and out.

As you breathe in try and imagine the room where you are eating. Look at the walls, the floor, the table. How dark or light is it in the room? Can you see what food is being served?

You have been invited to join Jesus at a dinner in the home of Simon the Pharisee, are there any other guests at the dinner?

Take in a deep breath and notice if you can smell anything in particular.

Then pay attention to what sounds you can hear coming from either inside or outside of the house.

As you sit lounging around the table, perhaps on a chair or on a couch, you decide to take a bite of the food that has been served. What can you taste? Can you see if Jesus is eating too?

As you begin to enjoy your meal, you notice a woman with long hair enter the room, carrying a small stone jar. Take a moment to really look at the woman, do you recognise her? What do you notice about her? How does she seem?

You watch as she walks directly toward Jesus who is lounging down to eat. As she walks you notice tears beginning to well up in her eyes.

How does Jesus respond to her? Does he say anything to the woman?

How does Simon react to her walking into his home uninvited?

You continue to watch as the woman approaches Jesus'. She is now crying heavily and you see her tears begin to fall upon Jesus' feet. You wonder what could possibly have happened to the poor woman to cause her such distress.

Reconciliation

She then bends down and begins patting Jesus' feet dry with her long hair. What are you thinking about as you watch her behave in this strange way.

How does Jesus appear to be feeling?

You then watch as the woman begins kissing Jesus' feet. As she does this you see her pour the contents of the stone jar over Jesus' feet.

You immediately recognise the smell of perfume. What does it smell like to you?

You turn in this moment to see Simon, quietly mumbling to himself. Look at his facial expressions, does he seem shocked, disgusted, or relaxed?

Jesus, also noticing Simon's reaction, turns to Simon and says, "Simon I have something to tell you."

Pay attention as Jesus tells Simon a story of a moneylender forgiving two people's debts, one for 500 silver coins and the other for 50. Jesus asks Simon which person would love the moneylender more.

You look over at Simon as he says "it would be the one who was forgiven more."

Jesus, while still talking to Simon, then turns to the woman at his feet and says:

"Do you see this woman? I came into your home, and you gave me no water for my feet, but she has washed my feet with her tears and dried them with her hair. You did not welcome me with a kiss, but she has not stopped kissing my feet since I came. You provided no olive oil for my head, but she has covered my feet with perfume. I tell you, then, the great love she has shown proves that her many sins have been forgiven."

You stare at Jesus, taking in all that he just said. Did he just say that her actions prove that her sins have been forgiven? What does that mean? Can Jesus forgive sins?

Has this woman brought her wrongdoings and brokenness to Jesus for healing?

Can I too bring my sins to Jesus to receive forgiveness?

Can I be healed?

As you question yourself you look over again at Simon. How do you think he is reacting to Jesus' words? Does he seem confused, annoyed, offended?

You take a moment to turn back toward Jesus and see him looking at the woman. You hear him say to her "Your sins are forgiven."

How does the woman respond to these words? How does she react to Jesus?

He then continues, by saying, "Your faith has saved you; go in peace."

You watch as the woman gets up and leaves the room. Notice how differently she seems as she leaves the room, compared to how she had entered earlier.

As you watch her depart you take in a final deep breath, noticing the lingering smell of perfume in the room.

The time has come to return to this room, so when you feel you are ready, begin by gently squeezing your hands, wriggling your toes, and then slowly start to open your eyes.

As you sit your bodies back up, we will say a short prayer of thanksgiving.

We thank you Holy Spirit for guiding our imaginations today and allowing us to experience God's word in this way.

I invite you now to speak aloud any prayers that you may like to share with the group.

Allow a moment for spontaneous prayer

Now that we have finished the meditation, I ask you to please move yourselves into a circle so that we can have a discussion about what you have just experienced in your imagination.

Discuss

1. Describe the scene as you sat sharing the meal with Simon and Jesus. What did you see, feel, smell, hear and taste?

2. What did you notice about the woman as she entered the room? How did Jesus and Simon respond to her?

3. What stood out to you about how the woman washed and anointed Jesus' feet? How were you feeling in that moment?

4. What did you think about the story Jesus told about the moneylender? How did that relate to the woman at Jesus' feet?

5. What do you think Jesus was trying to explain to Simon the Pharisee, and what could the message be for you?

Contemplate

Now to finish off we're going to take 10-15 minutes for contemplation, to really reflect upon this woman's encounter with Jesus. During this time you can respond to your imaginative prayer experience in a variety of different ways.

One response could be to write a recount or a snapshot describing in detail what you saw and felt during the imaginative prayer. A different written response might be to compose a prayer or write a letter to help you remember the experience at a later time. For those of you who would prefer to draw, focus your drawing on a specific moment within the imaginative prayer experience that stood out to you in a powerful or vivid way. During this time reflect on why you think Luke decided to include this particular story in his Gospel. Perhaps you could think about this woman's response to Jesus and the words that he spoke to her "Your sins are forgiven." What might God be trying to communicate to you through this scripture passage?

** Have some quiet reflective music playing in the background whilst children work**

Introduction to the Lost Parables

Crucial to Jesus' teaching on repentance and reconciliation are the three lost parables that are recorded in Luke's Gospel (Luke 15: 1-31). Jesus told these three parables together—the Lost Sheep, the Lost Coin, and the Lost Son—as a way of emphasising that God is merciful and celebrates our repentance. It is important, therefore, that the three passages are explored together, highlighting the differences and similarities between the parables.

Parables were a popular method of teaching in biblical times and you can find many examples of parables in both the New and the Old Testaments. A parable uses the tradition of storytelling to teach a particular message or truth that might be difficult for people to understand. By incorporating familiar life experiences into the story, a parable aims to communicate to the audience a complex reality which has several layers of meaning.

The three lost parables were told by Jesus to a group of scribes and pharisees. These were Jewish men who dedicated their lives to following, interpreting, and teaching God's Law, so that the wider Jewish community was better equipped and able to understand God's teaching.

There are key differences within the three lost parables that the educator should first understand before exploring them with students:
- The coin of the second parable is, evidently, an inanimate object. Although it is valuable (in this case it is worth approximately one day's wage) a coin clearly could not *choose* to be lost, nor would it *know* if it had been lost. As such the coin cannot in any way be deemed *responsible* for being lost.
- The sheep of the first parable, however, is alive and presumably has some ability to choose where it wanders. Similar to the coin, however, a sheep may not *know* that it is lost and it certainly cannot be *blamed* for not being able to find its way back to the shepherd.

- The lost son of the third parable, however, is different. The son is capable of making decisions for himself. He *chooses* to ask for his inheritance, he *chooses* to leave his family and to recklessly waste his money, he *chooses* (out of desperation) to go against the Jewish Law and find employment taking care of pigs, knowing this would almost completely sever his relationship with God.

In all of these stories, whether the "lost" were culpable or not, Jesus emphasises the celebration that follows when what was lost has been found.

One way to think about these three parables is that they can give us insight into different groups of people in our world today. Some people are like the lost coin, unaware of God's existence. Perhaps they have never been exposed to Christian teaching, and therefore cannot be blamed for their lack of relationship with God. In this instance, like the woman who searches for the coin, it is God who is constantly seeking to bring these people to Himself.

Other people may be similar to the lost sheep, unsure of where to go and which path to follow. They may not be concerned or even aware that they are lost. The lost sheep might refer to people who are searching for God but have no idea where to look. These are the people who need Jesus the Good Shepherd to find them and bring them to God.

Then there are others in our society, perhaps even some of us, who can relate to the lost son. Maybe having made a series of bad decisions these people now find themselves so far from God that they don't know how to turn back. It is through an understanding and acknowledgement of their sins, through repentance and a turning away from harmful behaviour, that the Father will not only welcome these people back with open arms, but will run towards them to celebrate their return.

One final, but important, point to note: parables are not ideal passages for using the imaginative prayer approach because they themselves are a teaching method, rather than an actual historical event that we can imagine being a part of. As such this book does not include an imaginative prayer experience for *The Lost Sheep,* nor *The Lost Coin.* Instead of using imaginative prayer, it is suggested that you explore these passages *before* reading the *Lost Son* and that you use other approaches to reading these scripture passages such as Lectio Divina, Godly Play, Bibliodrama or other methods that your students will find engaging.

The parable of the *Lost Son,* however, has been included in this resource due to its pertinence in understanding the Sacrament of Penance and Reconciliation. Due to the complexity of the story, and the need to allow students time to unpack the meaning of the parable for themselves, the story the *Lost Son* has been divided into two separate imaginative prayer experiences.

Reconciliation

The Lost Son

Part 1 - The Forgiving Father

Luke 15: 11-32 GNT Catholic Edition

Please ensure you have read the 'Introduction to the Lost Parables' BEFORE leading this Imaginative Prayer with children.

In today's imaginative prayer we will be focusing our attention on the first part of the Lost Son parable. We want to better understand the forgiveness of the father for his son. We will first begin by reading the entire passage together from the Bible before imagining the scene for ourselves.

Historical Context

This parable begins with a son asking for his share of his father's property. This share of the property is called an inheritance. Jesus' audience would have known that you could not *ask* for your share of your fathers inheritance, rather you receive your share *only* when your father dies. In fact, just to have asked would have been considered extremely rude, mean, and even shameful.

To the Jewish people who were listening to Jesus, they would have been outraged that the son had taken a job feeding pigs. This is because Jews considered pigs to be unclean animals. This meant that no one could touch them or eat any part of the animal, because to do so would make the person ritually unclean and they would no longer be in right relationship with God. Jesus would have chosen this job intentionally to emphasise to his Jewish audience just how desperate and far away from God this man had wandered. It would have seemed like nothing could save the son, that what he had done was unforgiveable. Yet Jesus tells us that not only did the father forgive him, but that he restored him to the role of son and celebrated his return. This would have been absolutely shocking to anyone who heard it!

Even the gifts that the Father gives the son on his return are significant. The robe and ring were both symbols of honour and authority. At the time family rings would have had an indentation on the top, an image or symbol that was unique to that particular family. The ring was then used like a signature, to identify the person and was used to put into wax to seal the back of a letter. This would have given the son the power to make decisions on behalf of the family.

Let us begin this session with a prayer of petition.
In the name of the Father, the Son, and the Holy Spirit.
Holy Spirit we ask that you help guide our thoughts and our imaginations during this time of prayer, Amen.

Encounter

Use a Bible to read the passage aloud to the class. Where possible, always allow students to hold their own Bible and to read along with you.

Now sit comfortably with your Bibles open to the Gospel of Luke within the New Testament and find the large number 15 which represents Chapter 15. Then find the small number 11 which is called the verse. I will be reading Luke 15: 11-32 aloud and I ask that you silently read along with me.

Read Luke 15: 11-32 through slowly, ensuring that students are reading along

The Lost Son
11 Jesus went on to say, "There was once a man who had two sons. 12 The younger one said to him, 'Father, give me my share of the property now.' So the man divided his property between his two sons. 13 After a few days the younger son sold his part of the property and left home with the money. He went to a country far away, where he wasted his money in reckless living. 14 He spent everything he had. Then a severe famine spread over that country, and he was left without a thing. 15 So he went to work for one of the citizens of

Reconciliation

that country, who sent him out to his farm to take care of the pigs. [16]He wished he could fill himself with the bean pods the pigs ate, but no one gave him anything to eat. [17]At last he came to his senses and said, 'All my father's hired workers have more than they can eat, and here I am about to starve! [18]I will get up and go to my father and say, "Father, I have sinned against God and against you. [19]I am no longer fit to be called your son; treat me as one of your hired workers."' [20]So he got up and started back to his father.

"He was still a long way from home when his father saw him; his heart was filled with pity, and he ran, threw his arms around his son, and kissed him. [21]"Father,' the son said, 'I have sinned against God and against you. I am no longer fit to be called your son.' [22]But the father called to his servants. 'Hurry!' he said. 'Bring the best robe and put it on him. Put a ring on his finger and shoes on his feet. [23]Then go and get the prize calf and kill it, and let us celebrate with a feast! [24]For this son of mine was dead, but now he is alive; he was lost, but now he has been found.' And so the feasting began.

[25]"In the meantime the older son was out in the field. On his way back, when he came close to the house, he heard the music and dancing. [26]So he called one of the servants and asked him, 'What's going on?' [27]'Your brother has come back home,' the servant answered, 'and your father has killed the prize calf, because he got him back safe and sound.' [28]The older brother was so angry that he would not go into the house; so his father came out and begged him to come in. [29]But he spoke back to his father, 'Look, all these years I have worked for you like a slave, and I have never disobeyed your orders. What have you given me? Not even a goat for me to have a feast with my friends! [30]But this son of yours wasted all your property on prostitutes, and when he comes back home, you kill the prize calf for him!' [31]'My son,' the father answered, 'you are always here with me, and everything I have is yours. [32]But we had to celebrate and be happy, because your brother was dead, but now he is alive; he was lost, but now he has been found.'"

When we read through for a second time we are only going to read part of the passage through, focusing on the son's return home. As we do that try and imagine the scene and what is happening in the story.

Read **Luke 15: 11-24** slowly to the class before guiding the students through the scene

Thank you for reading along. Now that you know the story I'd like you to place your Bibles down and find a comfortable place to lay down and close your eyes. We're now going to begin the meditation part of our prayer, where we allow the Holy Spirit to guide our imaginations. I will guide you through the process. Try to remain relaxed. If you get distracted, don't worry, just try and remain quiet and allow my voice to guide you back into your imagination.

Imagine

Let's begin by closing our eyes and taking in three slow deep breaths. Breathing in and out, in and out, in and out.

As you breathe in try and imagine yourself outside surrounded by a field. You have been out working in the field for the whole day. Take a moment to look around you and notice what the weather is like. Are there any other people working with you?

Take in a deep breath, are there any smells that you recognise?

Pay attention to what sounds you can hear as you work.

As you finish off your task for the day, you suddenly notice the owner of the property run out from his house. You watch him as he runs in your direction, heading towards the entrance to his property. You watch him wondering what he must be doing leaving in such a hurry. As he runs past you, notice his facial expression, does he seem stressed, excited, relieved?

Instinctively you turn towards the entrance gate, wondering what the owner must be running toward. As you look, you notice that there is a man coming the other way, walking towards the house. Take a moment to notice his appearance. Does he look tired, underfed, maybe even dirty? You strain your eyes to see his face more clearly and when you do, you suddenly recognise him as the owner's younger son. He looks so different but you are sure it must be him. You stare at him, even more confused. What would he be doing here? He left! And not only that, but he took his share of his father's inheritance with him when he went. Nobody takes their father's money when the father is still alive, it's like saying "I am no longer your son!"

Why would he return? He doesn't belong here anymore!

Reconciliation

Then you look again at the owner, his father. He is still running towards his son. You watch when the father finally reaches his son and embraces him.

How do you think the father feels as he hugs his son?

How do you think the son is feeling? Do either of them seem surprised, happy, concerned?

You hear the son say 'Father, I have sinned against God and against you. I am no longer fit to be called your son; treat me as one of your hired workers.'

The father pulls away from his son, notice his facial expression. Does he say anything in response to his son?

The father then turns and calls out, gesturing to his servants in the field.

'Hurry, bring the best robe and put it on him. Put a ring on his finger and shoes on his feet.'

You stand staring, unsure if you should be moving to help.

How can he be saying all of this? A robe…? A ring…?

The father then calls out again saying, 'Go and get the prize calf and kill it, and let us celebrate with a feast! For this son of mine was dead, but now he is alive; he was lost, but now he has been found.'

You turn and head toward the stable where the animals are resting. As you go you can't help but think about what the father just said. Why must everyone celebrate?

What does he mean that his son was lost but now is found?

You think about how much the father must love his son. It seems all of his bad behaviour has been forgiven.

Ask yourself, could I forgive like this father has forgiven?

The time has come to return to this room, so when you feel you are ready, begin by gently squeezing your hands, wriggling your toes, and then slowly start to open your eyes.

As you sit your bodies back up, we will say a short prayer of thanksgiving.

We thank you Holy Spirit for guiding our imaginations today and allowing us to experience God's word in this way.

I invite you now to speak aloud any prayers that you may like to share with the group.

Allow a moment for spontaneous prayer

Now that we have finished the meditation, I ask you to please move yourselves into a circle so that we can have a discussion about what you have just experienced in your imagination.

Discuss

1- Describe what the day was like whilst working out in the fields. What could you feel, hear, see, and smell?

2- Describe what you noticed about the son when you first recognised that it was him?

3- After they embraced, how do you think both the father and son were feeling?

4- How did you feel when the father said he wanted to shower his son with gifts?

5- What do you think Jesus was trying to teach his followers by telling this parable and what might his message be for you today?

Contemplate

Now to finish off we're going to take 10-15 minutes for contemplation, to really reflect upon this parable and the characters of the father and the younger son. During this time you can respond to your imaginative prayer experience in a variety of different ways. One response could be to write a recount or a snapshot describing in detail what you saw and felt during the imaginative prayer. A different written response might be to compose a prayer or write a letter to help you remember the experience at a later time. For those of you who would prefer to draw, focus your drawing on a specific moment within the imaginative prayer experience that stood out to you in a powerful or vivid

Reconciliation

way. As you reflect, in whatever way you would like, think about Jesus' message of forgiveness and reconciliation in this parable. Think about the mercy of the forgiving father, what could this teach us about God's mercy for us?

** Have some quiet reflective music playing in the background whilst children work**

The Lost Son

Part 2 - The Older Brother

Luke 15: 11-32 GNT Catholic Edition

** Ensure you have completed Part 1 "The Lost Son: The Forgiving Father" before leading this imaginative prayer experience**

In today's imaginative prayer we will be focusing our attention on the second part of the Lost Son parable. We want to better understand the older brother, the one who remained at home with his father. We will first begin by reading the passage together from the Bible before imagining the scene for ourselves.

Historical Context

The parable of the Lost Son is the last of the three lost parables that were taught by Jesus.

The character of the older brother in this parable is believed to represent the Pharisees, the people Jesus was speaking to when he told this story. The Pharisees were a group of religious Jews who strictly followed Jewish laws and customs, especially when it came to cleanliness and purity.

The father's complete forgiveness for his returning younger son would have seemed totally undeserved, even unjust, to the Pharisees who were listening to Jesus. Therefore, it is through the older brother's eyes that we can better understand how radical Jesus' message of mercy and complete forgiveness might have been for the audience at the time.

Reconciliation

Let us begin this session with a prayer of petition.

In the name of the Father, the Son, and the Holy Spirit.

Holy Spirit we ask that you help guide our thoughts and our imaginations during this time of prayer, Amen.

Encounter

Use a Bible to read the passage aloud to the class. Where possible, always allow students to hold their own Bible and to read along with you.

Now sit comfortably with your Bibles open to the Gospel of Luke within the New Testament and find the large number 15 which represents Chapter 15. Then find the small number 11 which is called the verse. I will be reading Luke 15: 11-32 aloud and I ask that you silently read along with me.

Read Luke 15: 11-32 through slowly, ensuring that students are reading along

The Lost Son

[11] Jesus went on to say, "There was once a man who had two sons. [12] The younger one said to him, 'Father, give me my share of the property now.' So the man divided his property between his two sons. [13] After a few days the younger son sold his part of the property and left home with the money. He went to a country far away, where he wasted his money in reckless living. [14] He spent everything he had. Then a severe famine spread over that country, and he was left without a thing. [15] So he went to work for one of the citizens of that country, who sent him out to his farm to take care of the pigs. [16] He wished he could fill himself with the bean pods the pigs ate, but no one gave him anything to eat. [17] At last he came to his senses and said, 'All my father's hired workers have more than they can eat, and here I am about to starve! [18] I will get up and go to my father and say, "Father, I have sinned against God and against you. [19] I am no longer fit to be called your son; treat me as one of your hired workers."' [20] So he got up and started back to his father.

"He was still a long way from home when his father saw him; his heart was filled with pity, and he ran, threw his arms around his son, and kissed him. ²¹"Father," the son said, 'I have sinned against God and against you. I am no longer fit to be called your son.' ²²But the father called to his servants. 'Hurry!' he said. 'Bring the best robe and put it on him. Put a ring on his finger and shoes on his feet. ²³Then go and get the prize calf and kill it, and let us celebrate with a feast! ²⁴For this son of mine was dead, but now he is alive; he was lost, but now he has been found.' And so the feasting began.

²⁵"In the meantime the older son was out in the field. On his way back, when he came close to the house, he heard the music and dancing. ²⁶So he called one of the servants and asked him, 'What's going on?' ²⁷'Your brother has come back home,' the servant answered, 'and your father has killed the prize calf, because he got him back safe and sound.' ²⁸The older brother was so angry that he would not go into the house; so his father came out and begged him to come in. ²⁹But he spoke back to his father, 'Look, all these years I have worked for you like a slave, and I have never disobeyed your orders. What have you given me? Not even a goat for me to have a feast with my friends! ³⁰But this son of yours wasted all your property on prostitutes, and when he comes back home, you kill the prize calf for him!' ³¹"My son,' the father answered, 'you are always here with me, and everything I have is yours. ³²But we had to celebrate and be happy, because your brother was dead, but now he is alive; he was lost, but now he has been found.'"

We are going to read part of the passage through one more time, focussing on the older brother. This time as we read through, I want you to try and imagine the scene and what is happening in the story

Read **Luke 15: 25-32** slowly to the class before guiding the students through the scene

Thank you for reading along. Now that you know the story I'd like you to place your Bibles down and find a comfortable place to lay down and close your eyes. We're now going to begin the meditation part of our prayer, where we allow the Holy Spirit to guide our imaginations. I will guide you through the process. Try to remain relaxed. If

Reconciliation

you get distracted, don't worry, just try and remain quiet and allow my voice to guide you back into your imagination.

Imagine

Let's begin by closing our eyes and taking in three slow deep breaths. Breathing in and out, in and out, in and out.

As you breathe in try and imagine yourself outside in a field. Take a moment to look around you. Notice whether the sun is shining or if there are clouds overhead.

As you look around the field, notice how many other people are also out there working. Notice what sounds you can hear. Perhaps you can hear the sounds of birds overhead or maybe there are people nearby talking to one another. Can you talk to anyone?

Take in another deep breath and notice what smells are in the air. Then as you begin to move your hand through the crop you look up and notice the older brother hard at work. What stands out to you about him? Perhaps it is his clothing, or his behaviour, or maybe how people are treating him.

As the day's work comes to an end and you begin to walk up towards the house with the other workers. As you walk you take in a deep breath, can you smell that there is a feast being prepared?

Notice what you can hear. Can you hear sounds of people celebrating? Perhaps you can hear the sound of people dancing, singing, or laughing. Can you hear any music playing, if so what kind of music?

You look over and notice once again the older brother. He has clearly heard the sound of the celebrations coming from the house. How does he seem? Does he look angry, happy, or maybe confused?

As you approach the house you notice a servant walking towards you and the other workers. You hear the servant announce that the younger brother has returned and that the fattened calf has been killed.

How does the older brother react to this news? Does he seem annoyed, shocked, upset? Are you able to go over and talk to him? If so, what is he saying?

You look up and now see that the father is coming out of the house walking toward his elder son. Pay attention to what the father is wearing? Can you see his facial expression, if so does he seem happy, excited, concerned?
What words can you hear him say to his son?

Watch as the son listens to his father, what does he say in response? Does he seem hurt, frustrated, or sad? You watch on as he tells to his father that he works like a slave, yet never has he even received a goat to celebrate with his friends.
What do you notice of the father's expression? How does he seem listening to his son react in this way? Does he appear calm, frustrated, tired?
Pay close attention to the tone used by the father as he speaks. "My son, you are always here with me, and everything I have is yours. But we had to celebrate and be happy, because your brother was dead, but now he is alive; he was lost, but now he has been found."

Take your time to rest here in the scene, move around, taking in all that you see, hear, touch and smell. Watch to see what the brother does in response to his father's plea. How might the older brother be feeling? How are you feeling in this moment?
Notice where the father is right now? Has he returned to the party?

When you feel like you have finished within the scene, think about how the story might end. What does the older son choose to do? Does he join the celebrations or does he decide to do something else? Think about what you might have done in the older brother's position. What can you learn from these characters that could help you in your own life?
The time has come to return to this room, so when you feel you are ready, begin by gently squeezing your hands, wriggling your toes, and then slowly start to open your eyes.

Reconciliation

As you sit your bodies back up, we will say a short prayer of thanksgiving.

We thank you Holy Spirit for guiding our imaginations today and allowing us to experience God's word in this way.

I invite you now to speak aloud any prayers that you may like to share with the group.

Allow a moment for spontaneous prayer

Now that we have finished the meditation, I ask you to please move yourselves into a circle so that we can have a discussion about what we just experienced in our imaginations.

Discuss

1- What could you see, feel, smell and hear while out in the fields?

2- How did the brother react when he heard from the servant about the celebration going on inside the house?

3- How did the father seem when he tried to convince his son to join the celebrations and how did the son react?

4- What did the brother decide to do at the end of the scene?

5- What do you think Jesus was trying to teach the Pharisees by sharing this parable?

Contemplate

Now to finish off we're going to take 10-15 minutes for contemplation, to really reflect upon this parable and the characters of the father and the older son. During this time you can respond to your imaginative prayer experience in a variety of different ways. One response could be to write a recount or a snapshot describing in detail what you saw and felt during the imaginative prayer. A different written response might be to compose a prayer or write a letter to help you remember the experience at a later time. For those of you who would prefer to draw, focus your drawing on a specific moment within the imaginative prayer experience that stood out to you in a powerful or vivid way. As you reflect, in whatever way you would like, think about what God might be trying to tell you through this parable? Why do you think Jesus told this story and what might the message be for you hearing it today?

*** Have some quiet reflective music playing in the background whilst children work***

www.ingramcontent.com/pod-product-compliance
Lightning Source LLC
Chambersburg PA
CBHW041711290426
44109CB00028B/2842